We are a collective of artists who share a passion for creating fun and relaxing coloring books. Hours of work went into creating this - we really hope you have lots of fun with it.

Copyright and Trademarks

All rights reserved. This book or any portion thereof may not be reproduced or used in any manner whatsoever without the express written permission of the publisher except for the use of brief quotations in a book review.

First printing, Nov 2020
Copyright © 2020

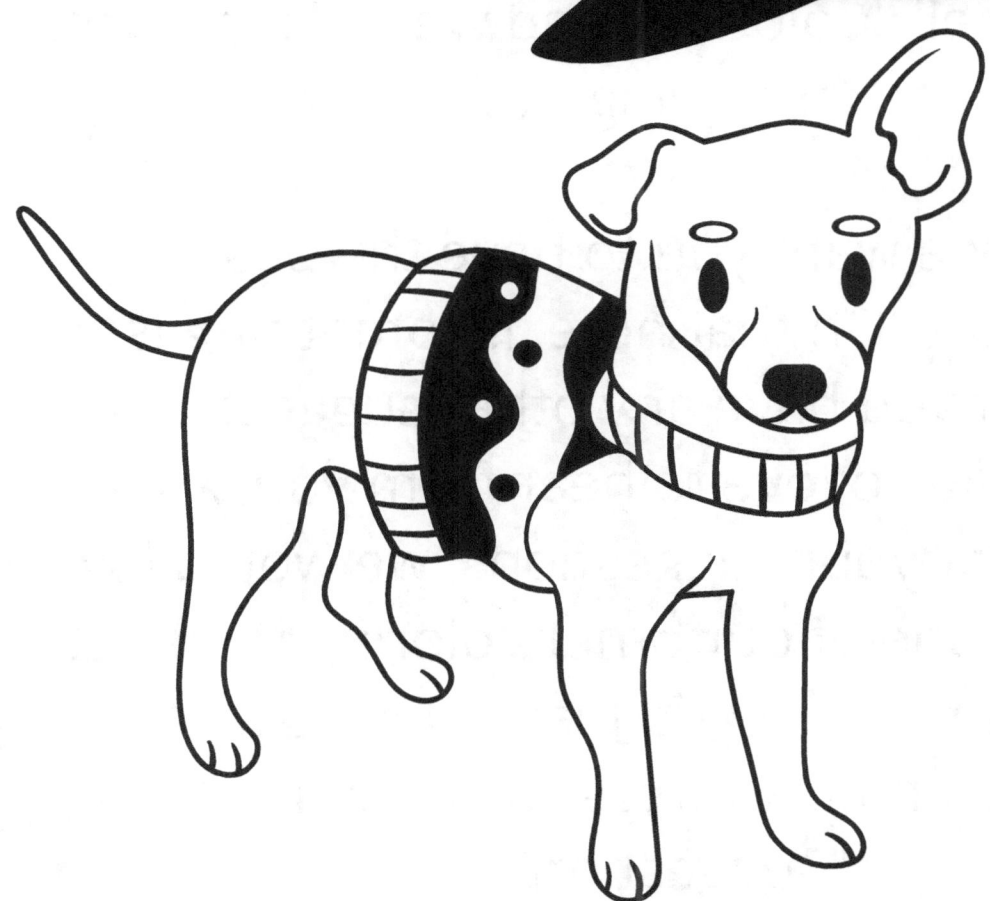

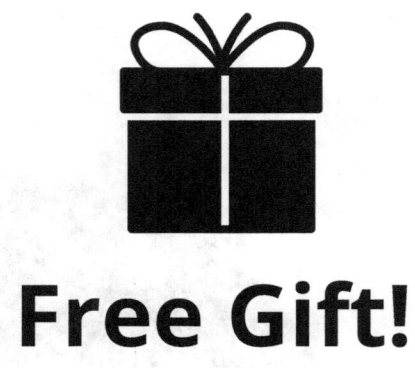

Free Gift!

Want a free gift?

Email us at painttherapydesigns@gmail.com

Title the email "Coloring" and we will send you something fun!

Also, we want you to have the best experience. On that note, if something is amiss or if you have any other suggestions, we would also love to hear from you. As a thank you for your suggestions, we would love to give you one of our other coloring books as a complementary gift! Just email us at the same email address with the title "Suggestion".

Tips for Coloring

There are no hard and fast rules when it comes to coloring, but here are some tips that can help:
- Using color pencils? Then make sure to sharpen your pencil more than you think you need to.
- Using markers or gel pens? Always test them on the Color Test page in the front to check if it bleeds through or leaves a shadow.
- Don't worry about going outside the lines. It is perfectly fine. You can even color all over the page - there are no rules you need to stick to. Let your imagination go wild!
- Don't rush. Take your time with your coloring. The point is to relax and enjoy yourself, don't worry about finishing them fast. Just enjoy yourself and you will be happier with your colorings.

Most importantly, have fun!

LET THE FUN BEGIN!

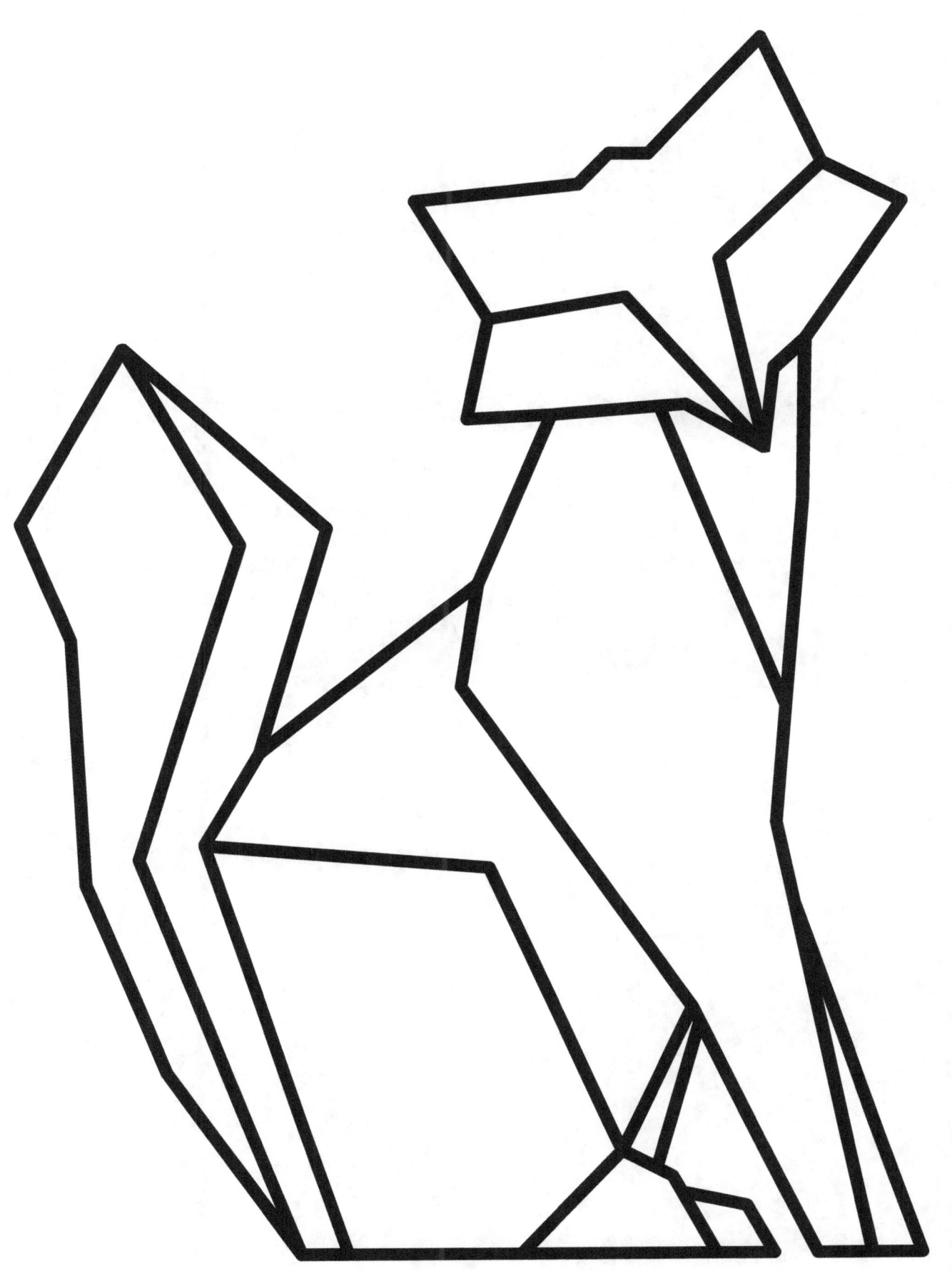

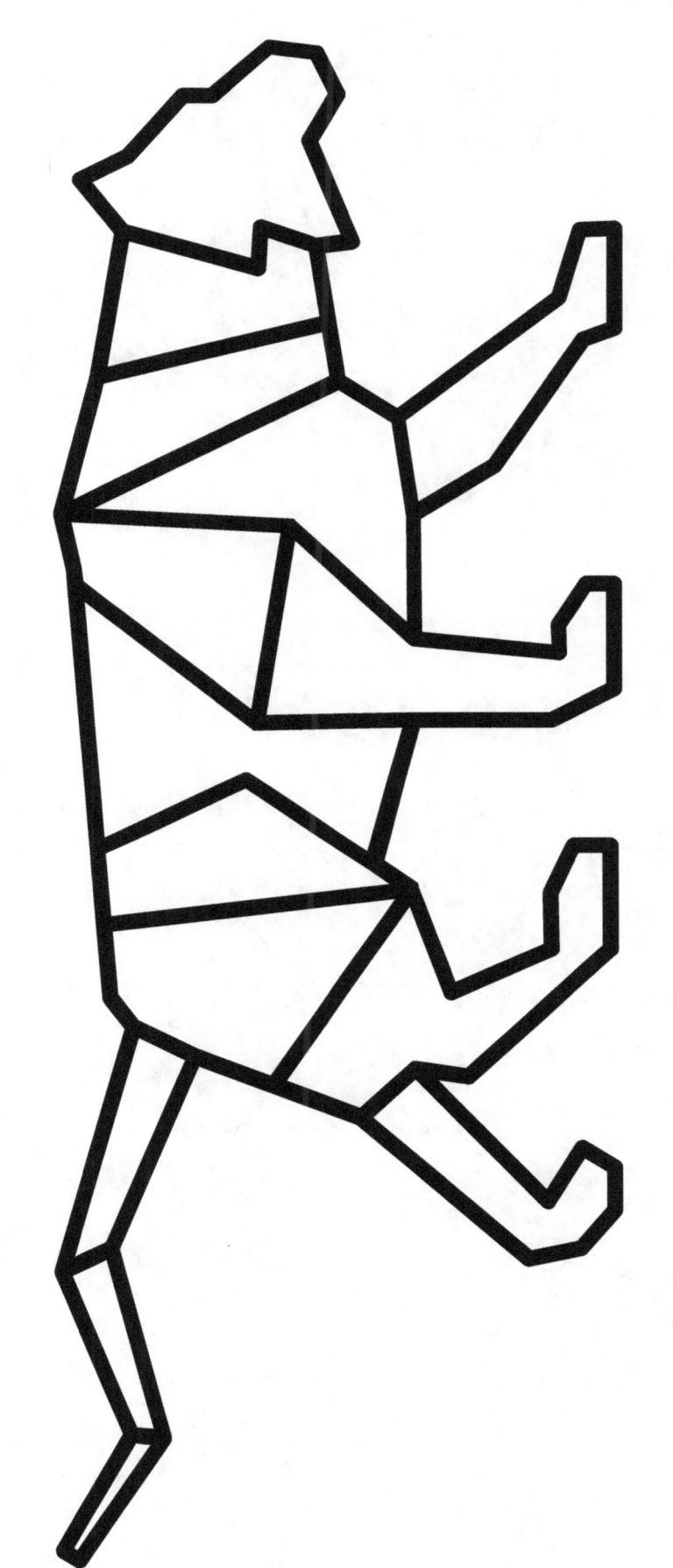

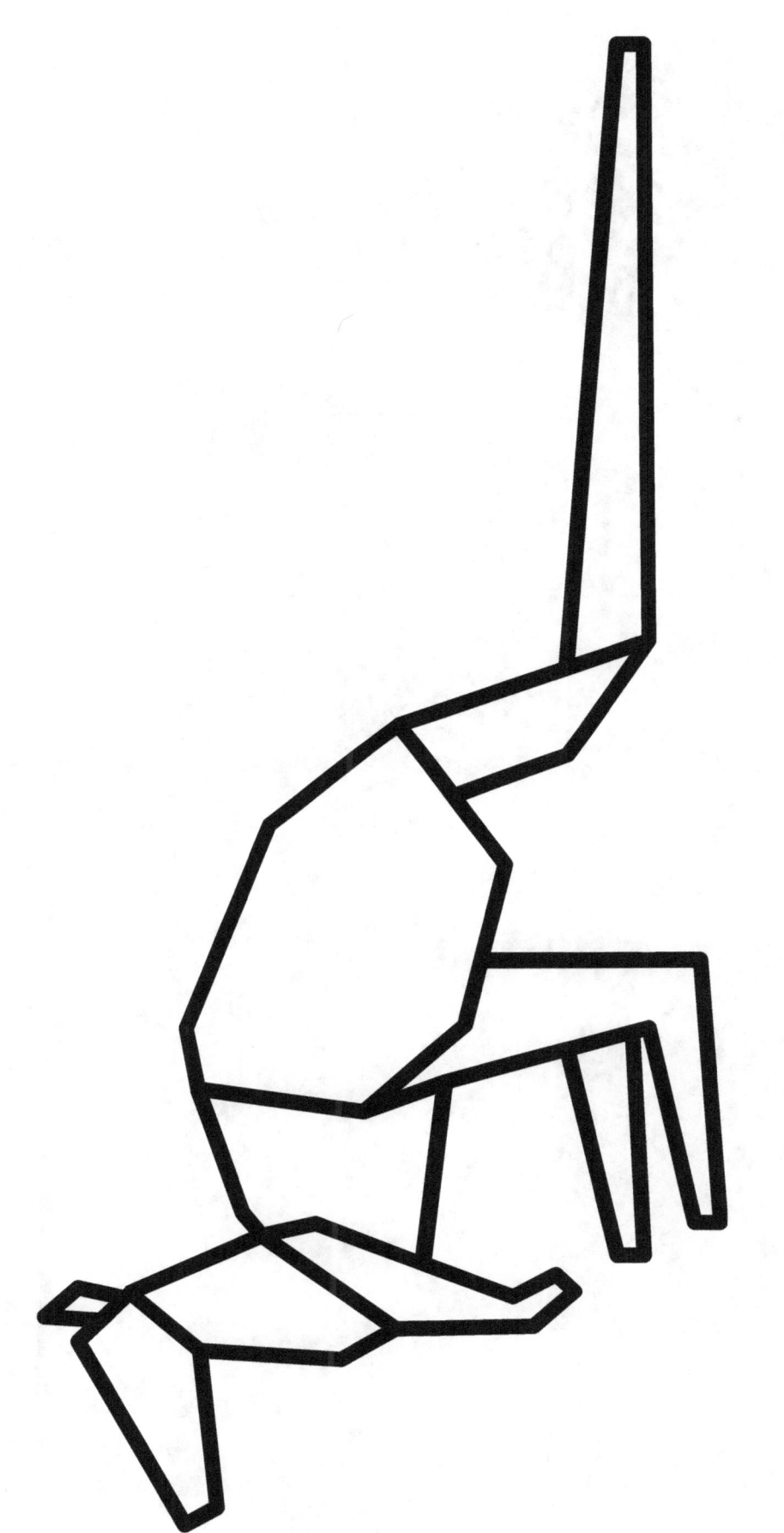

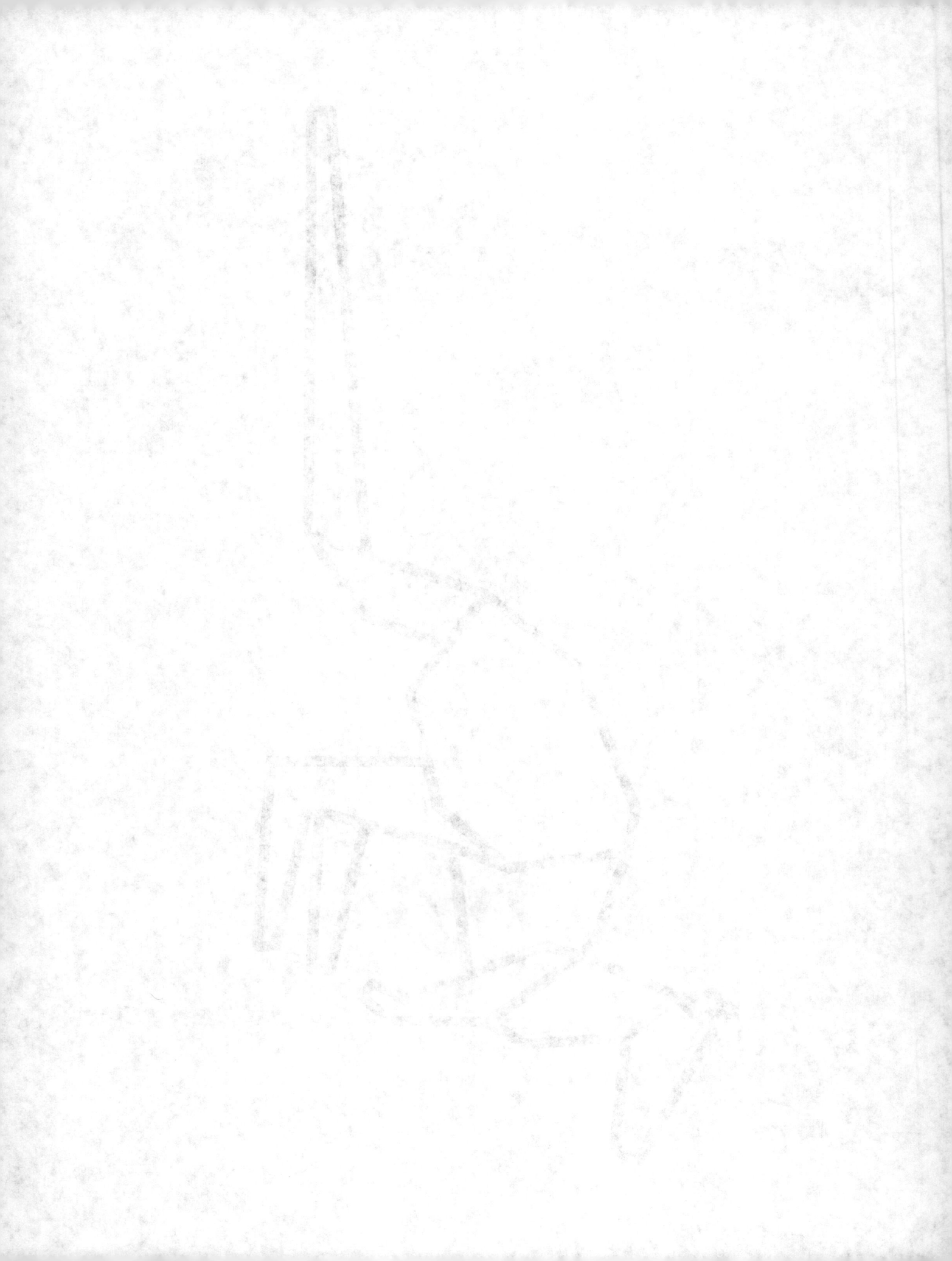

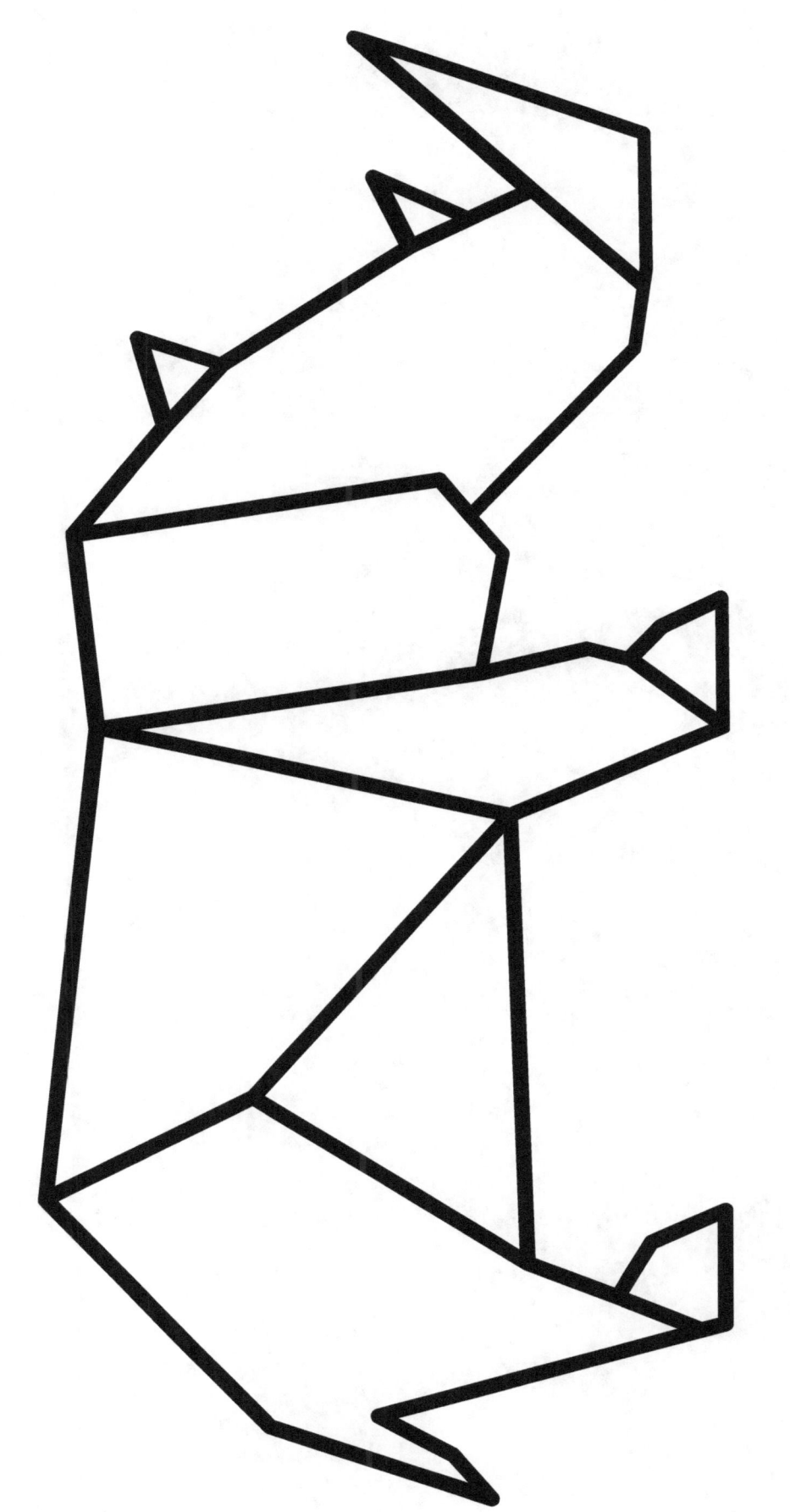

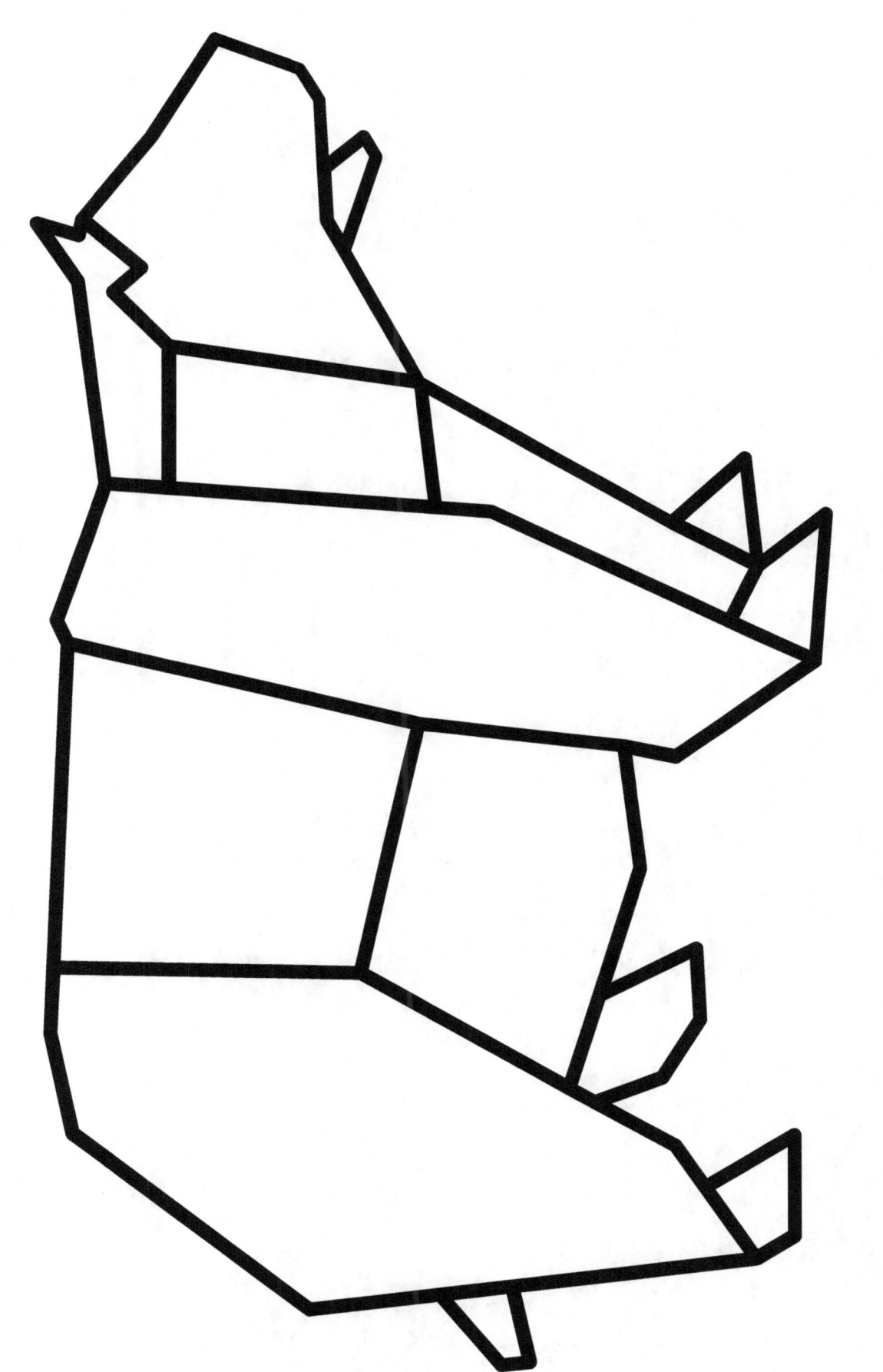

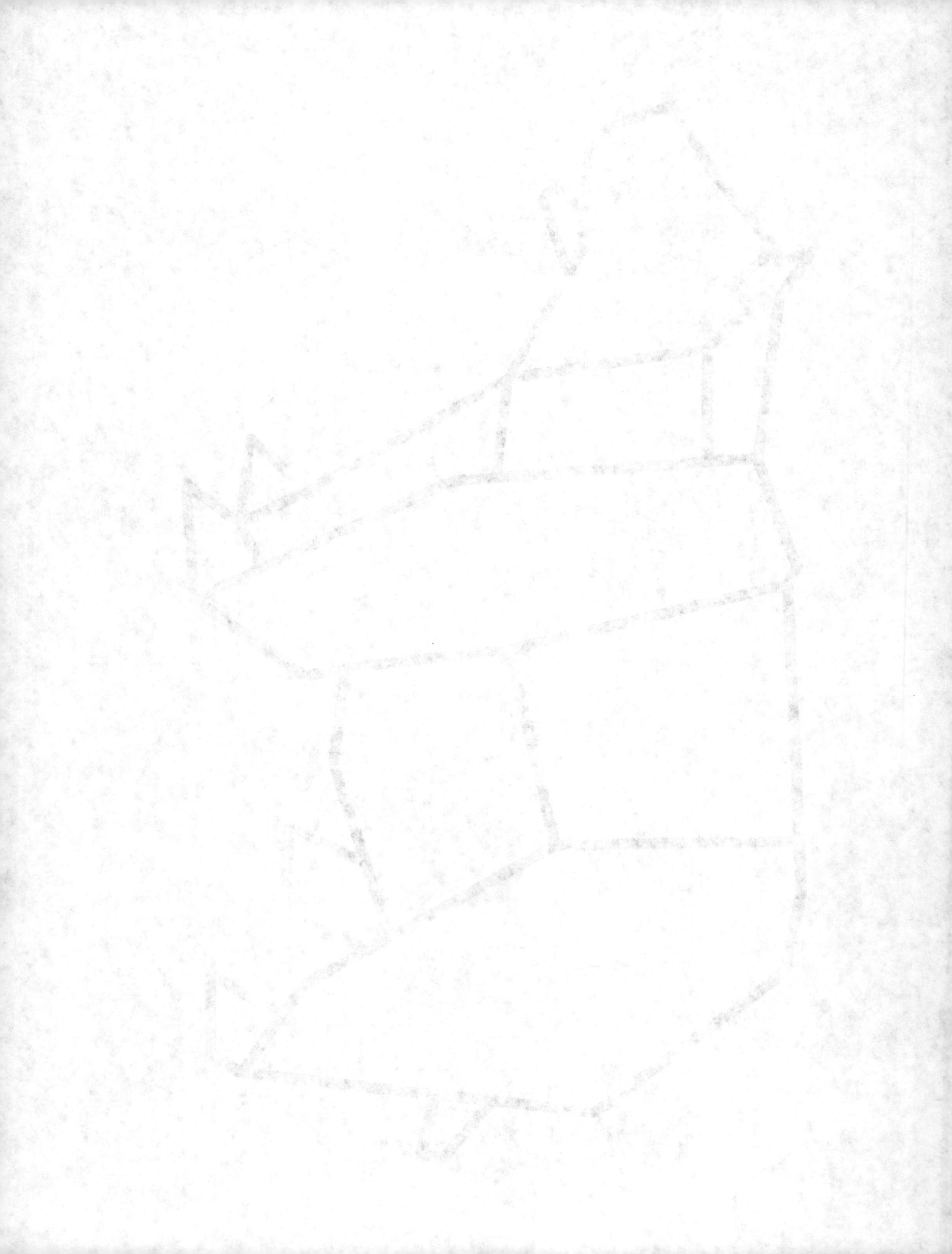

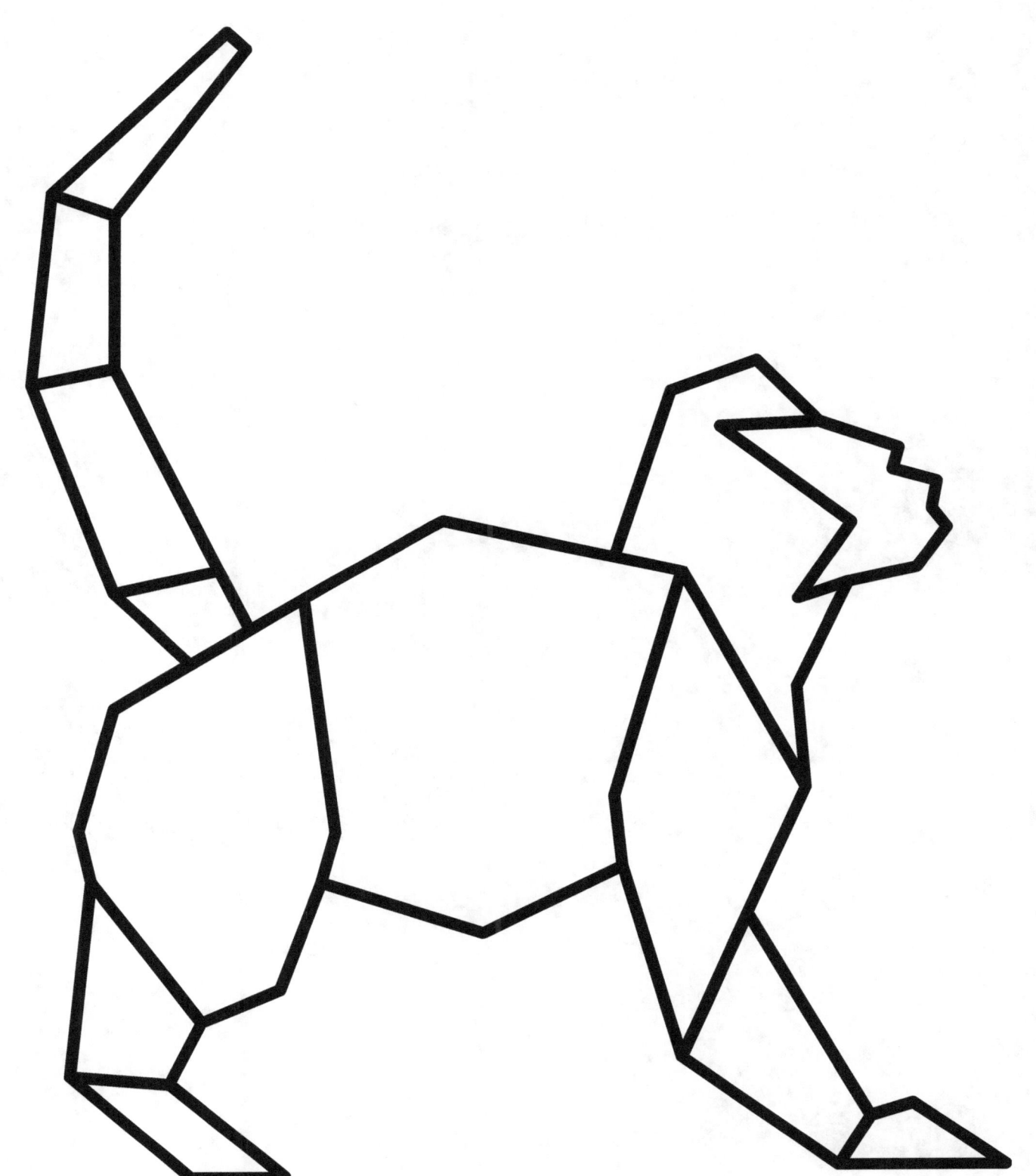

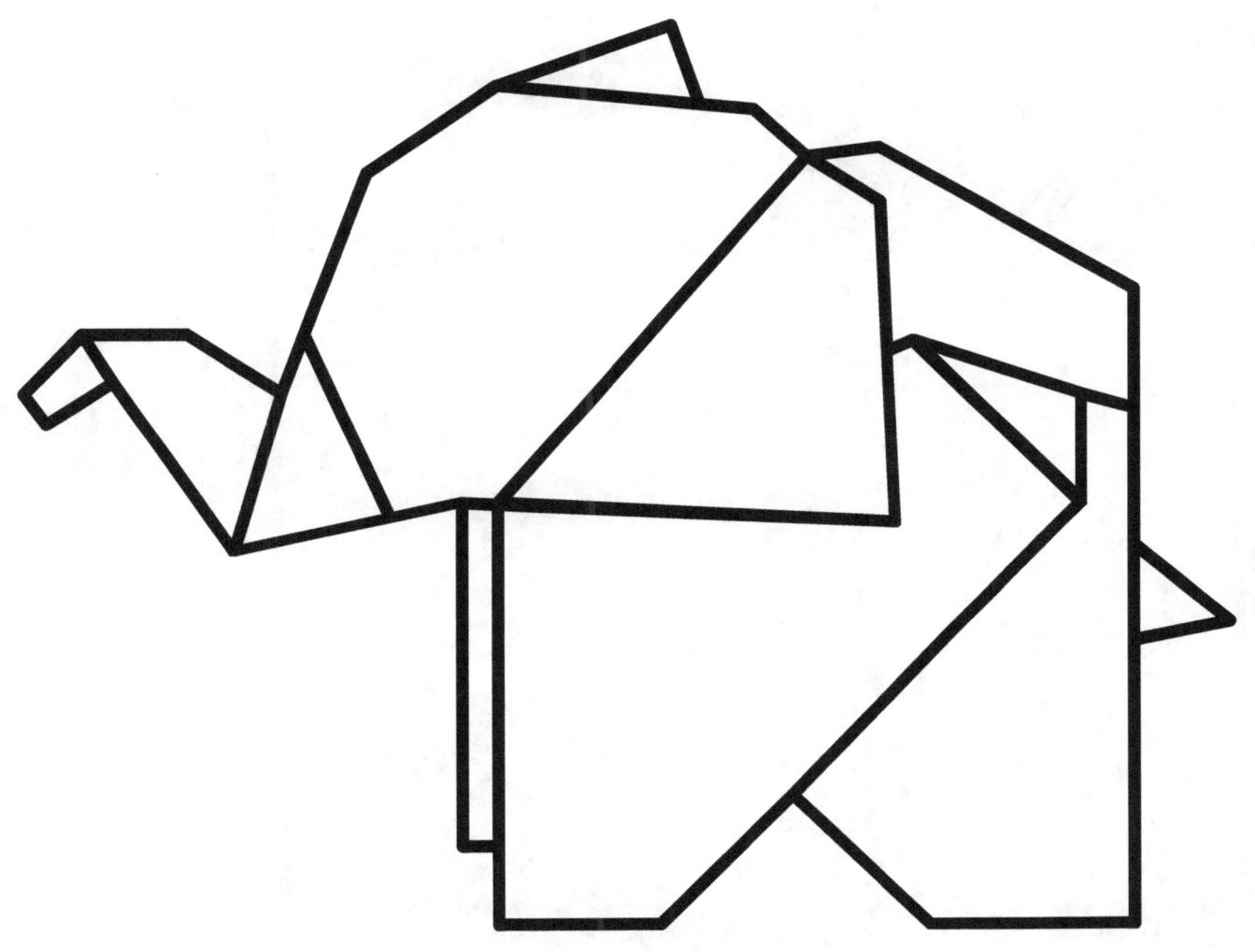

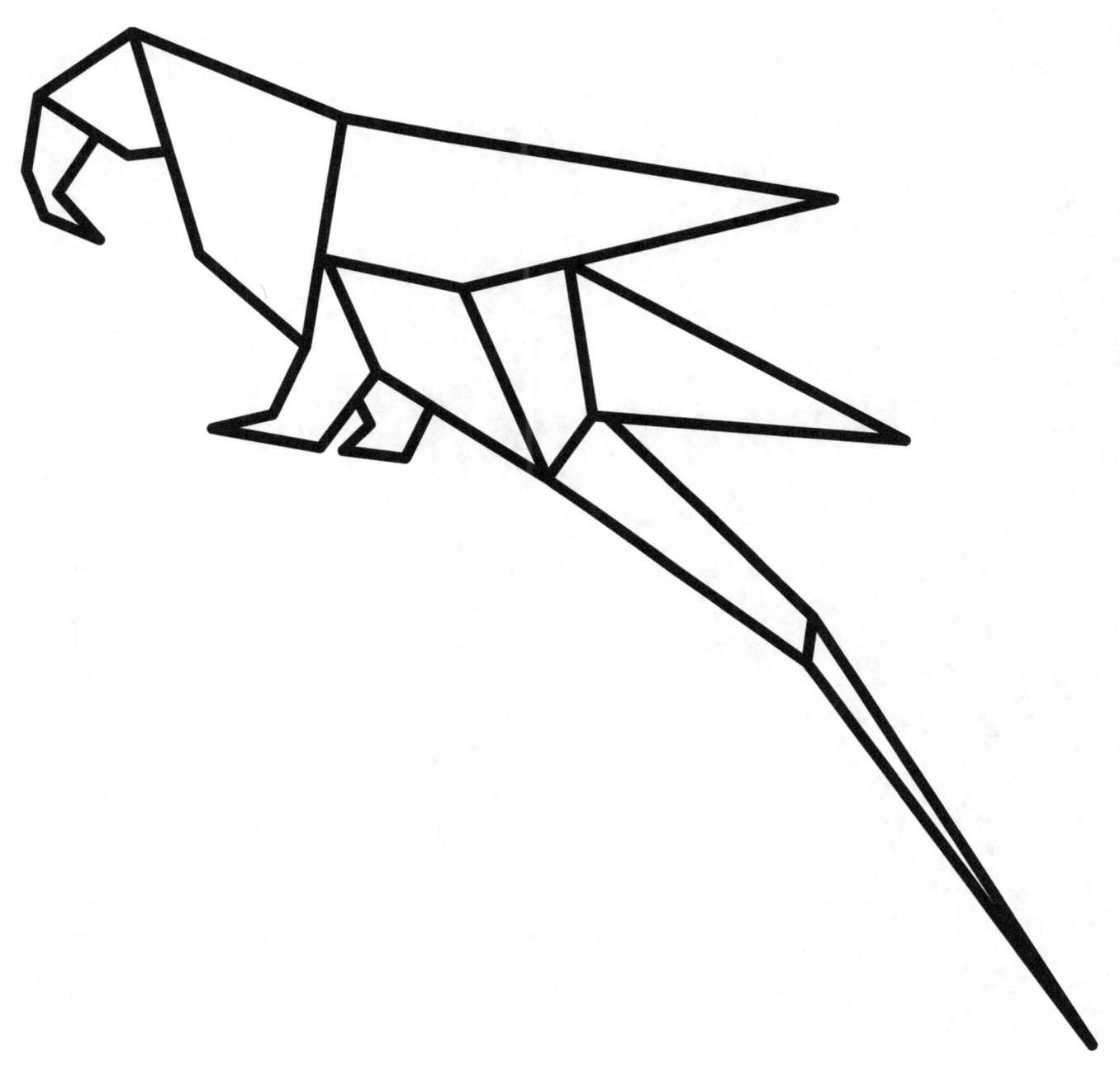

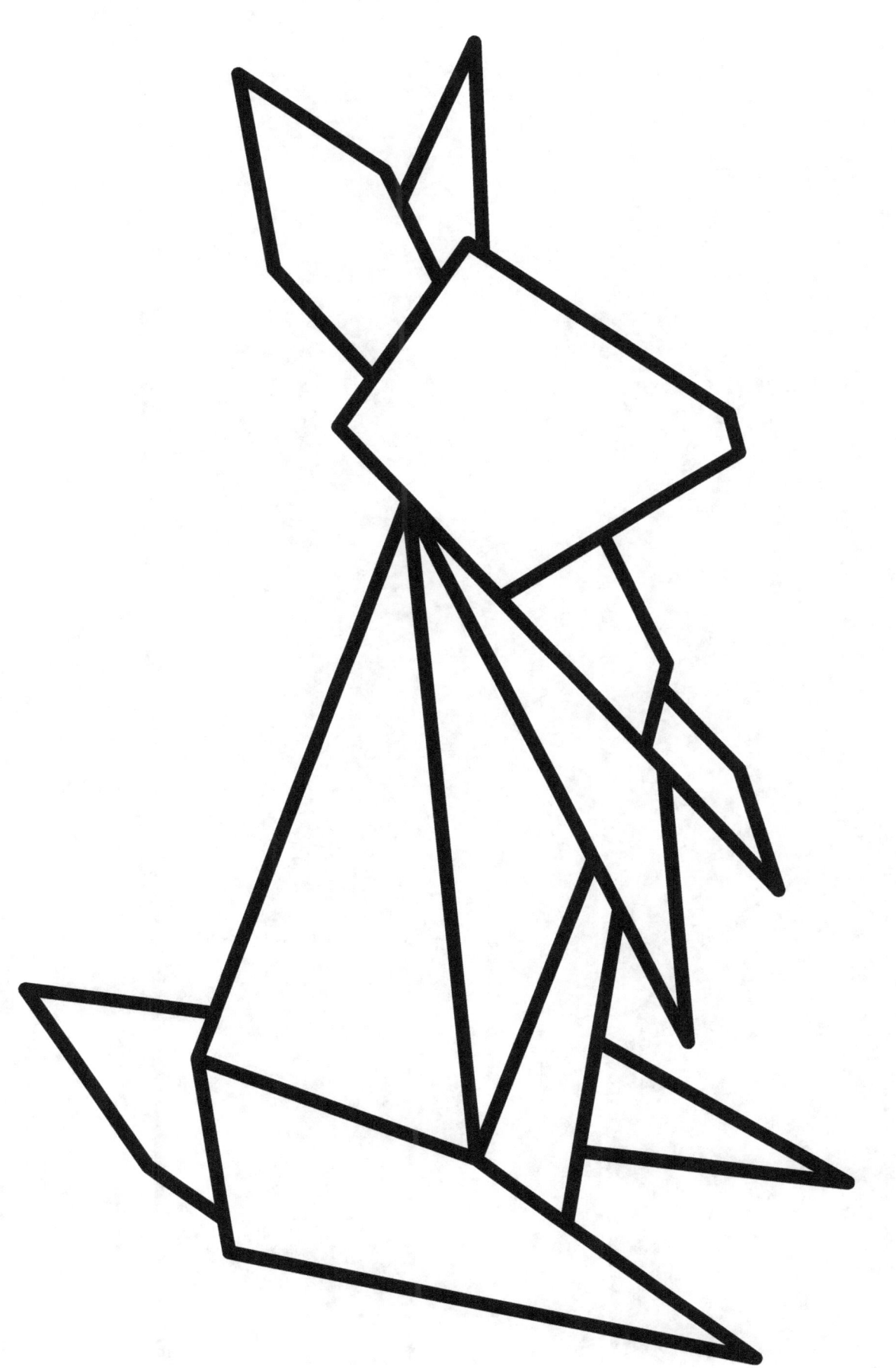

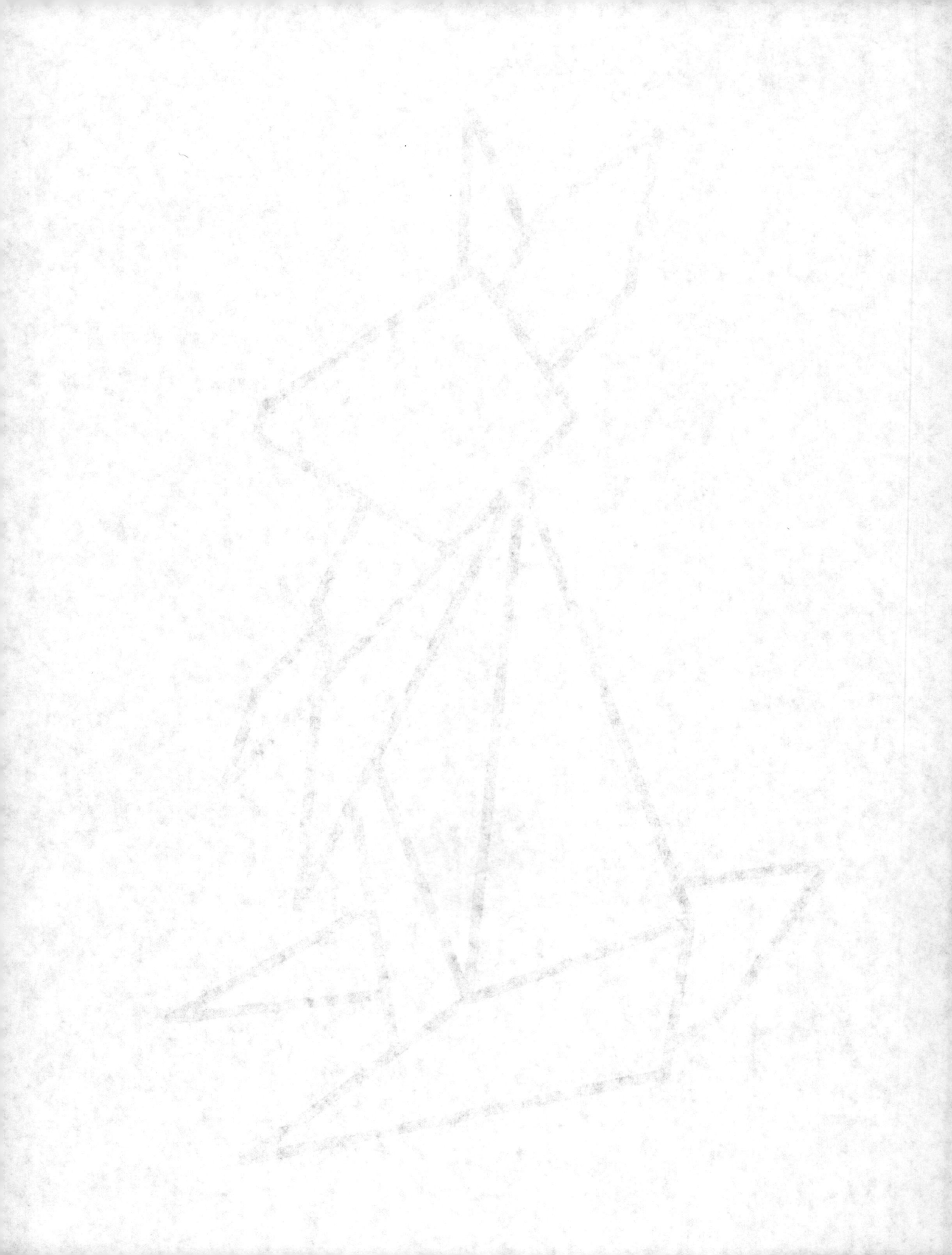

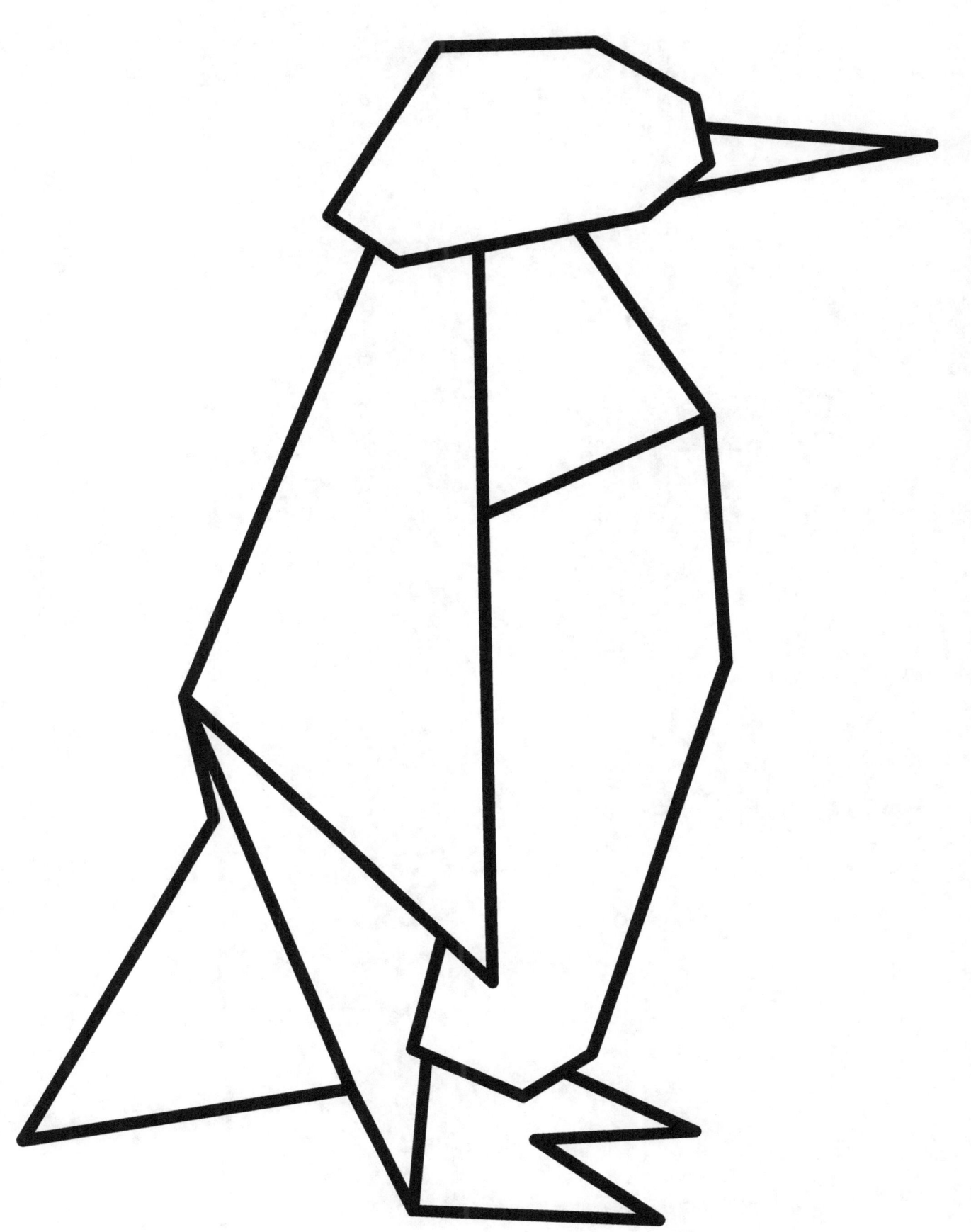

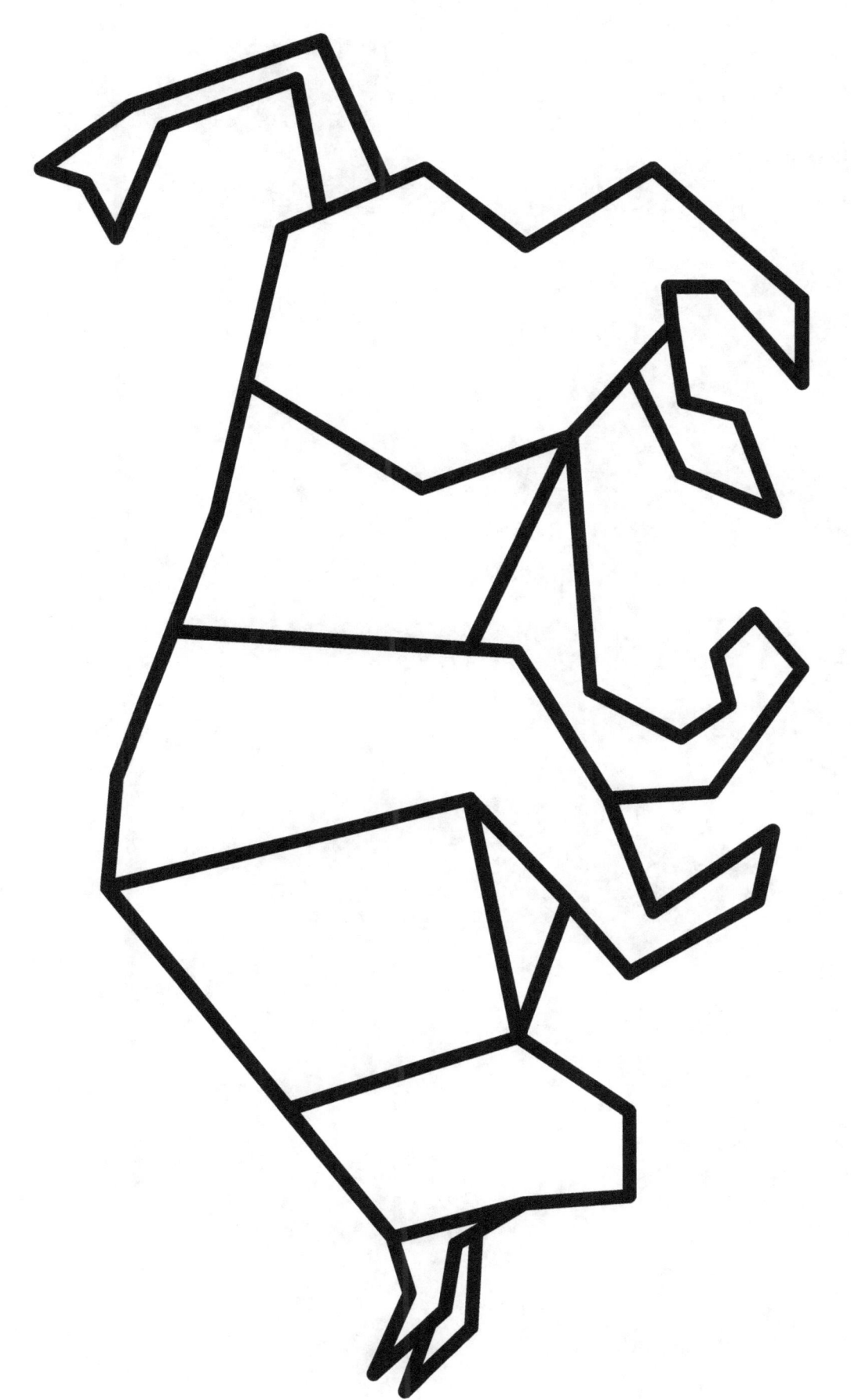

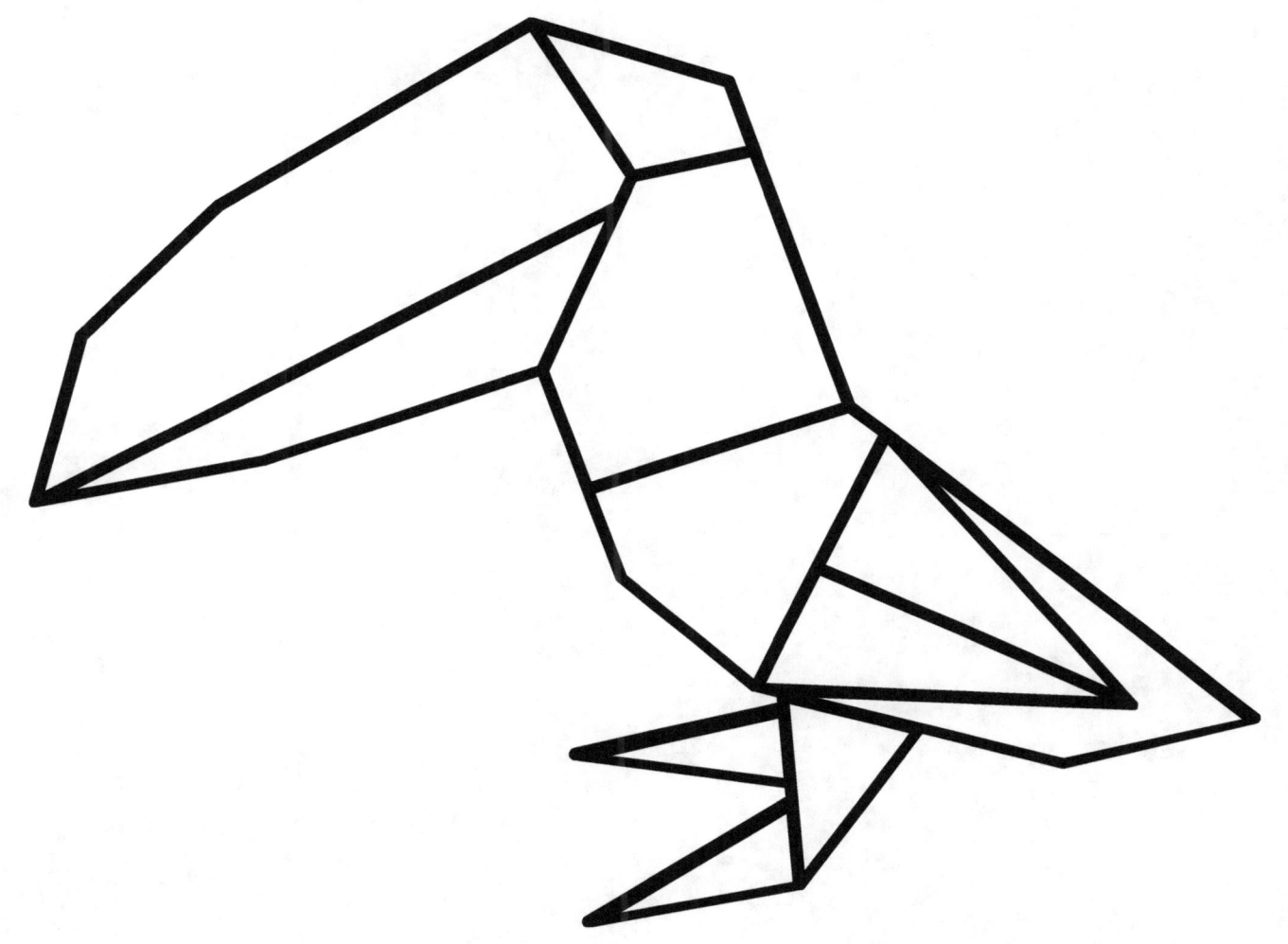

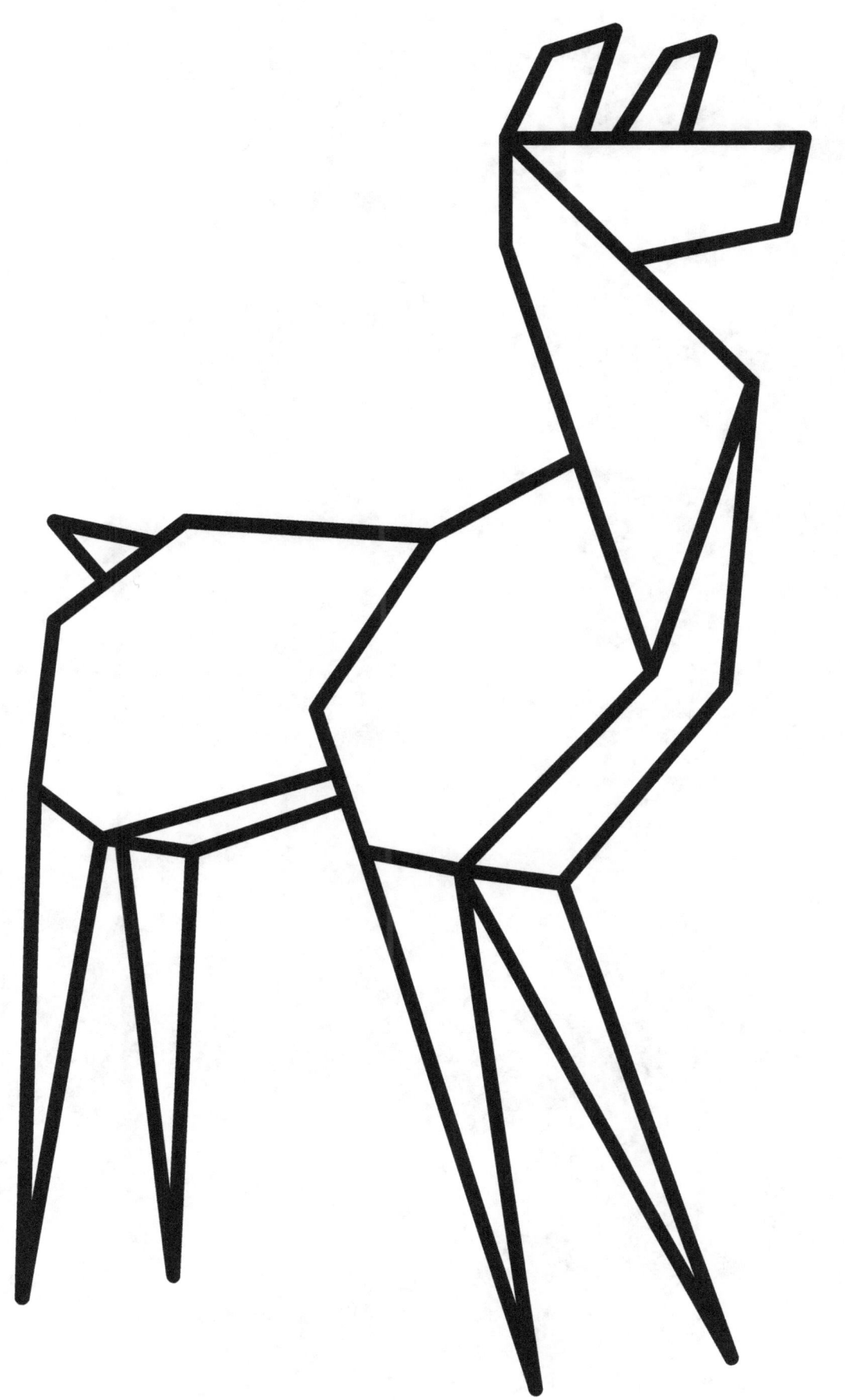

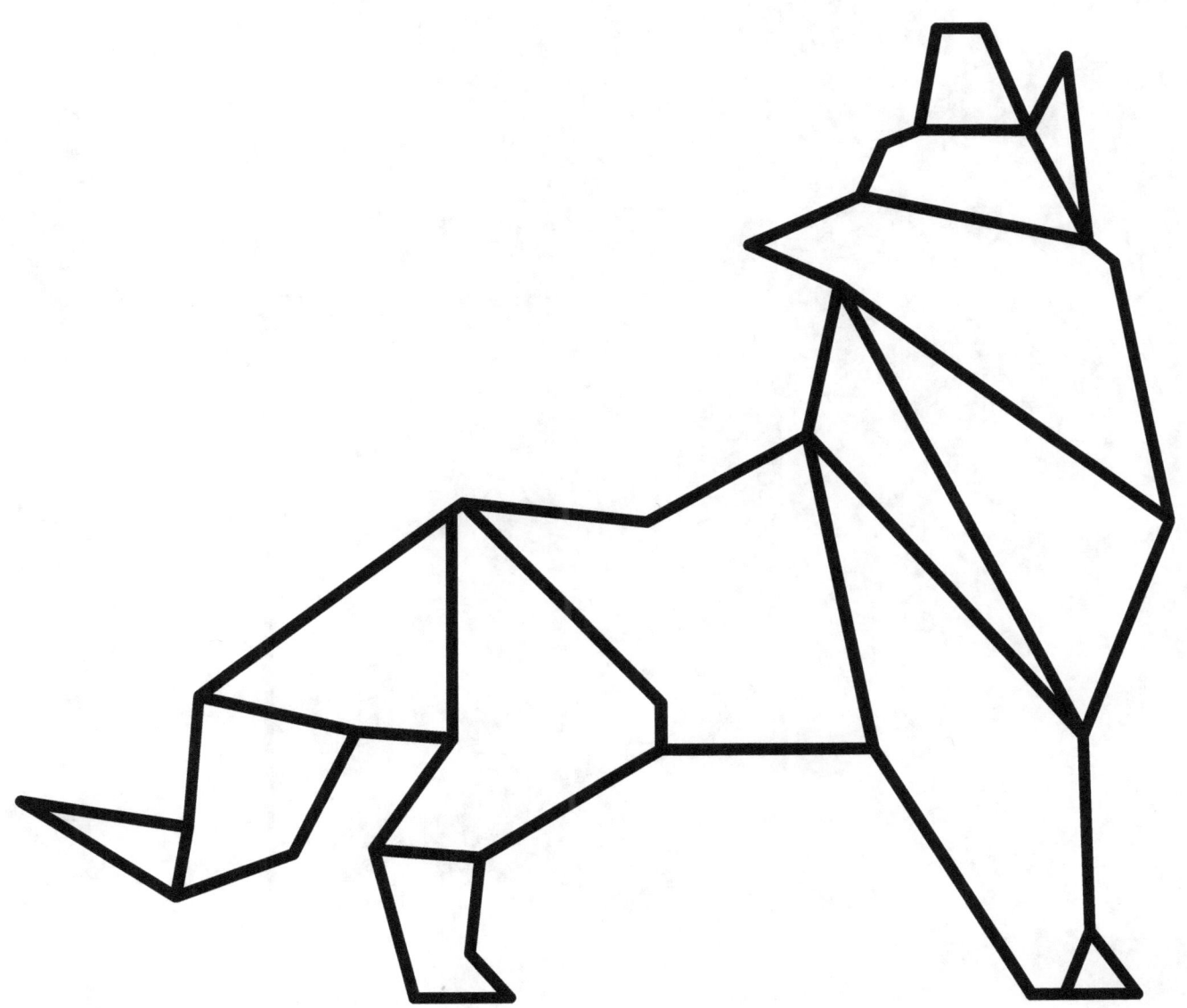

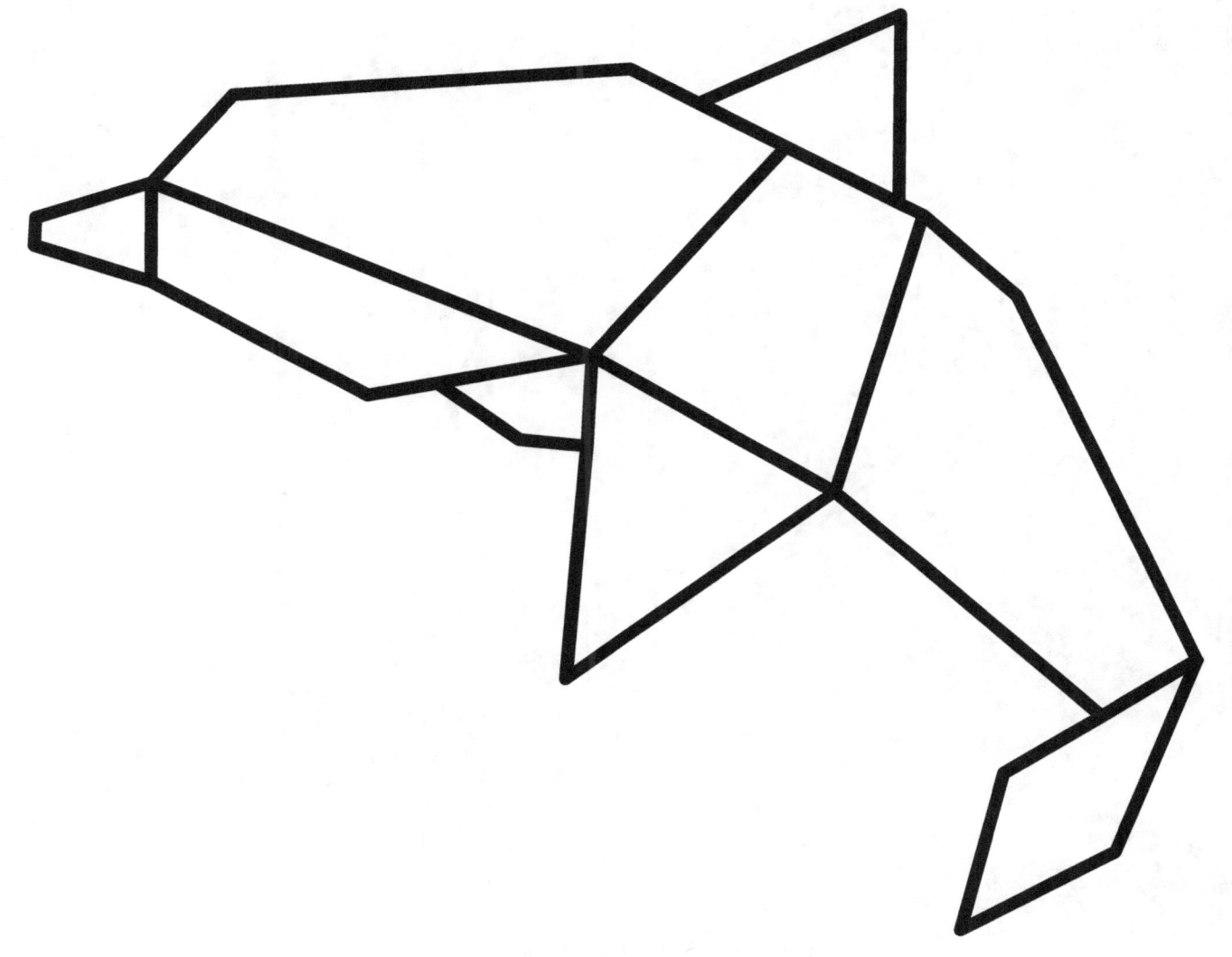

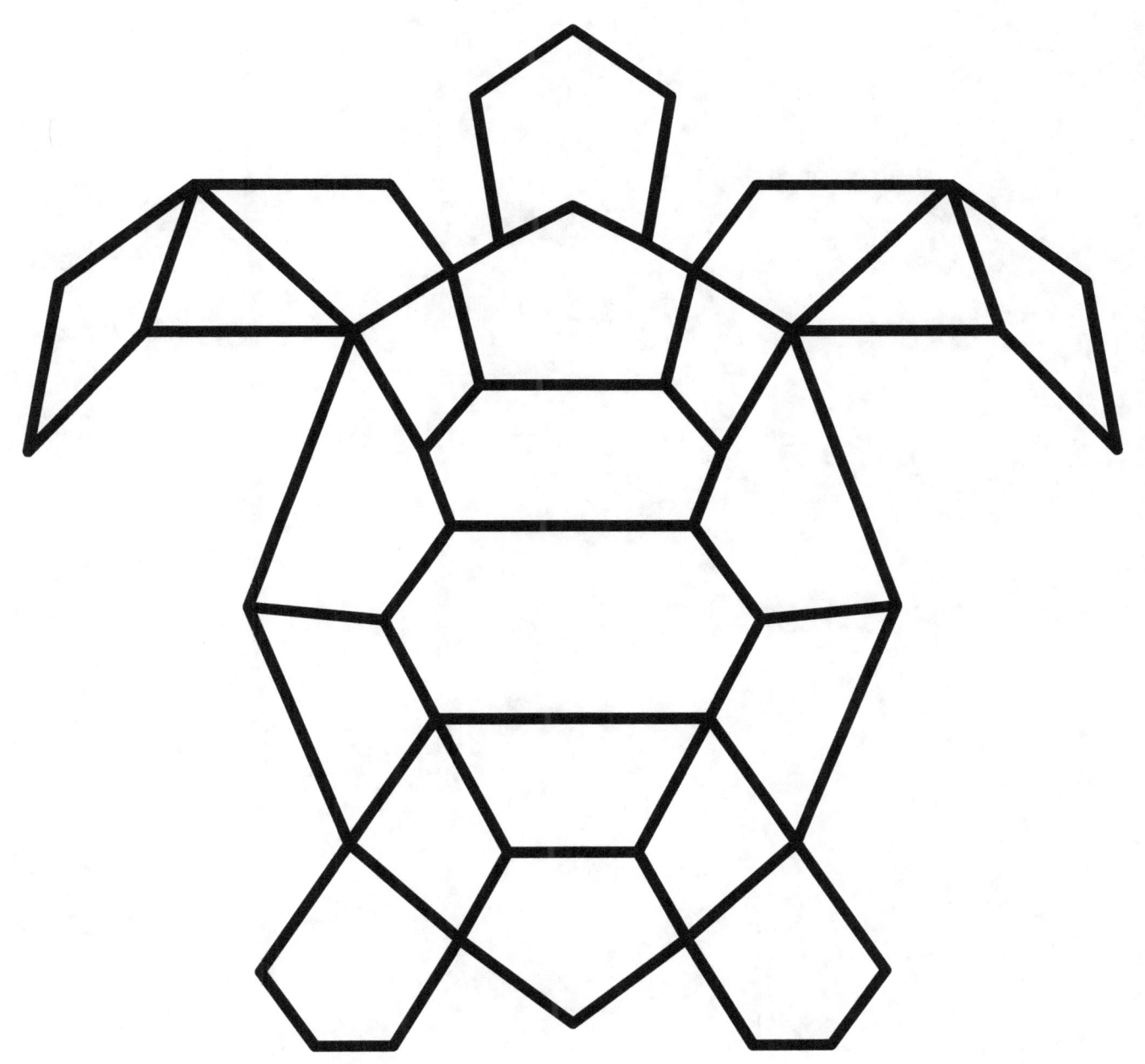

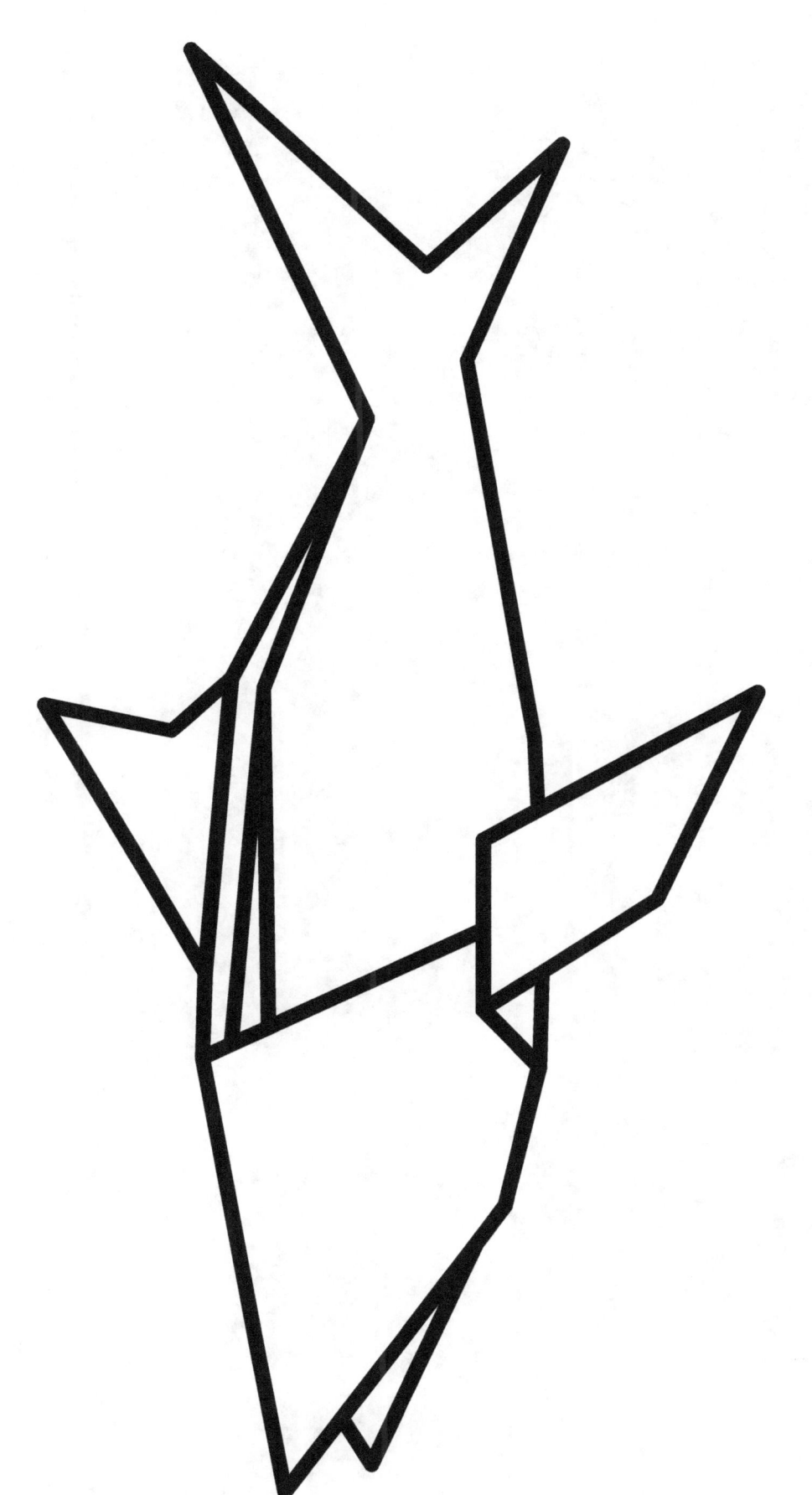

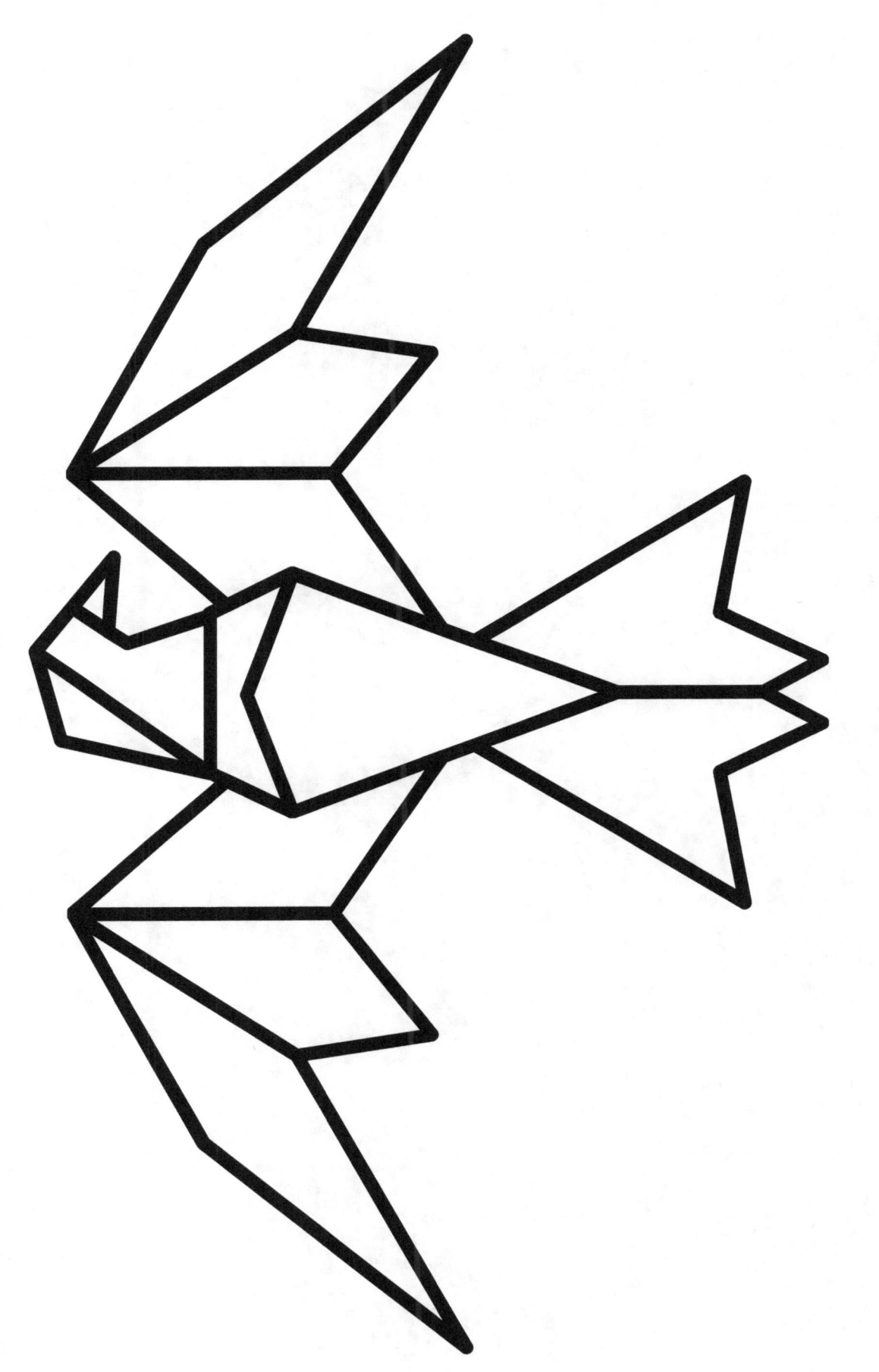

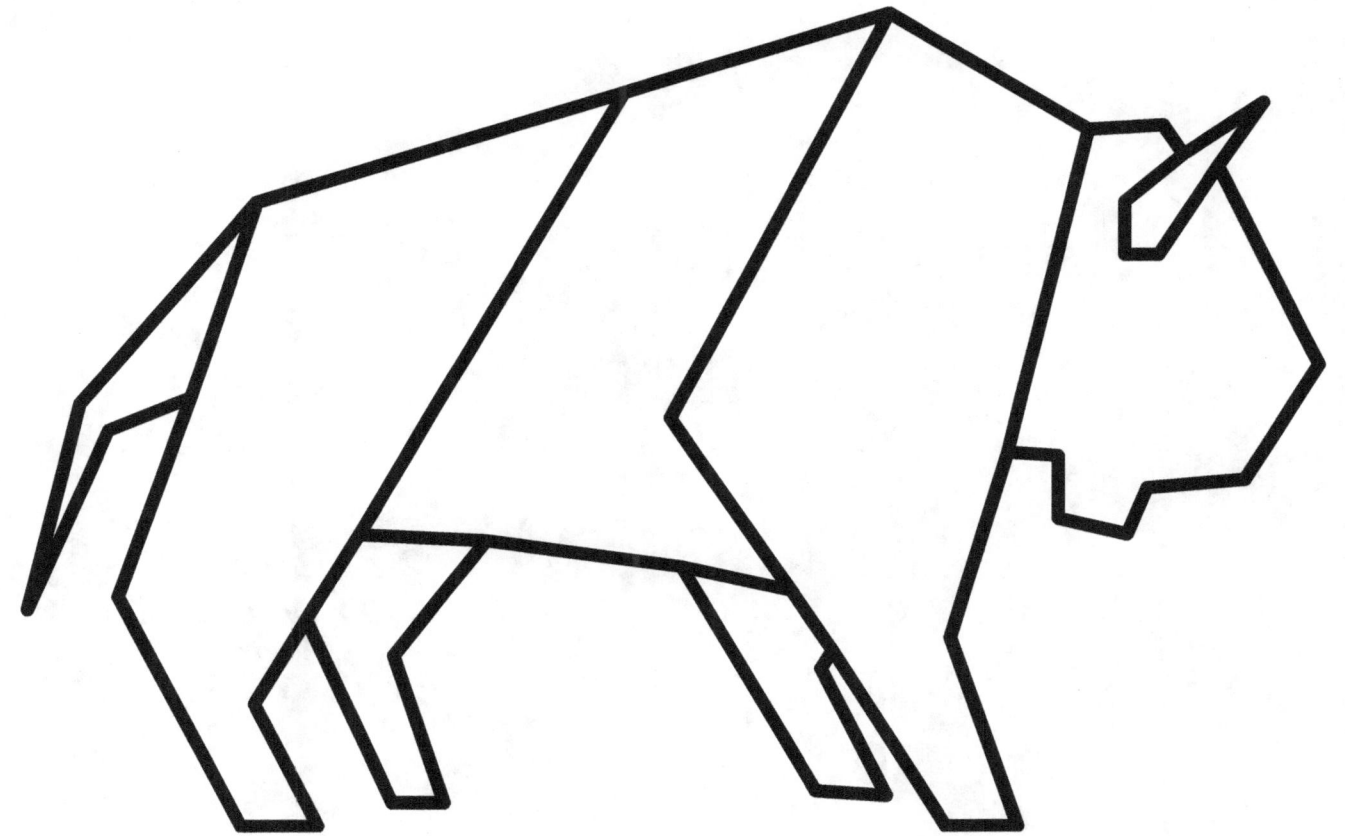

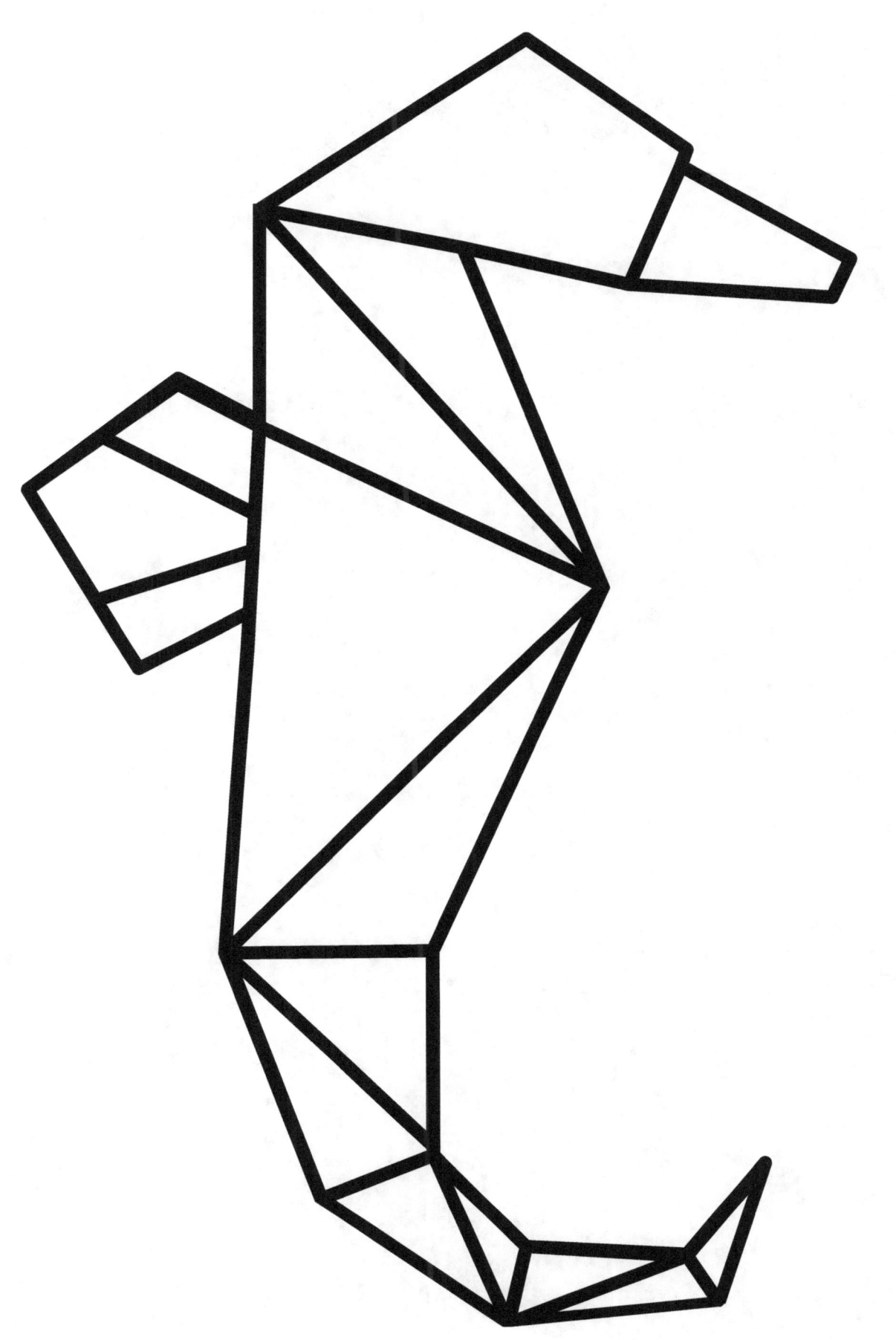

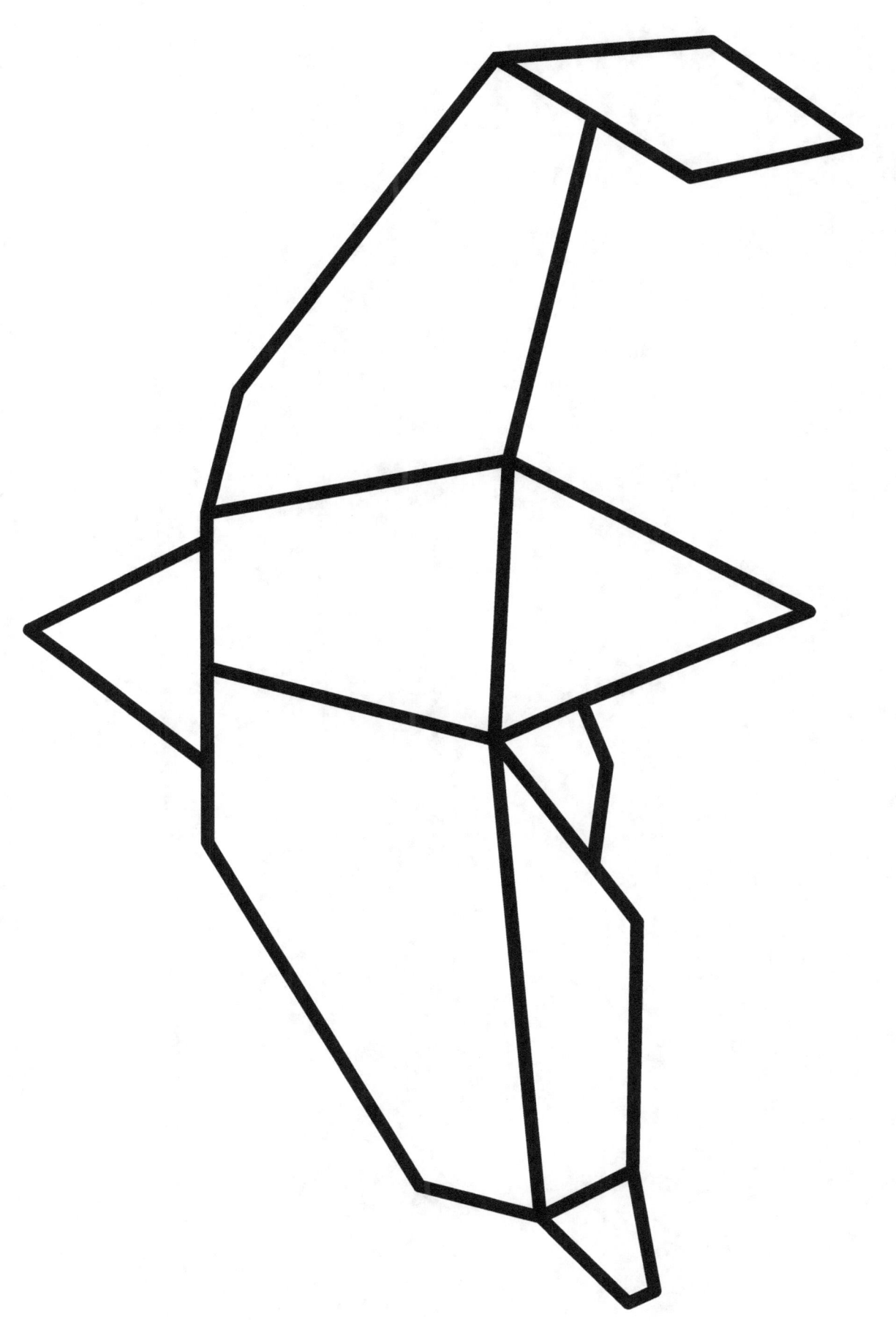

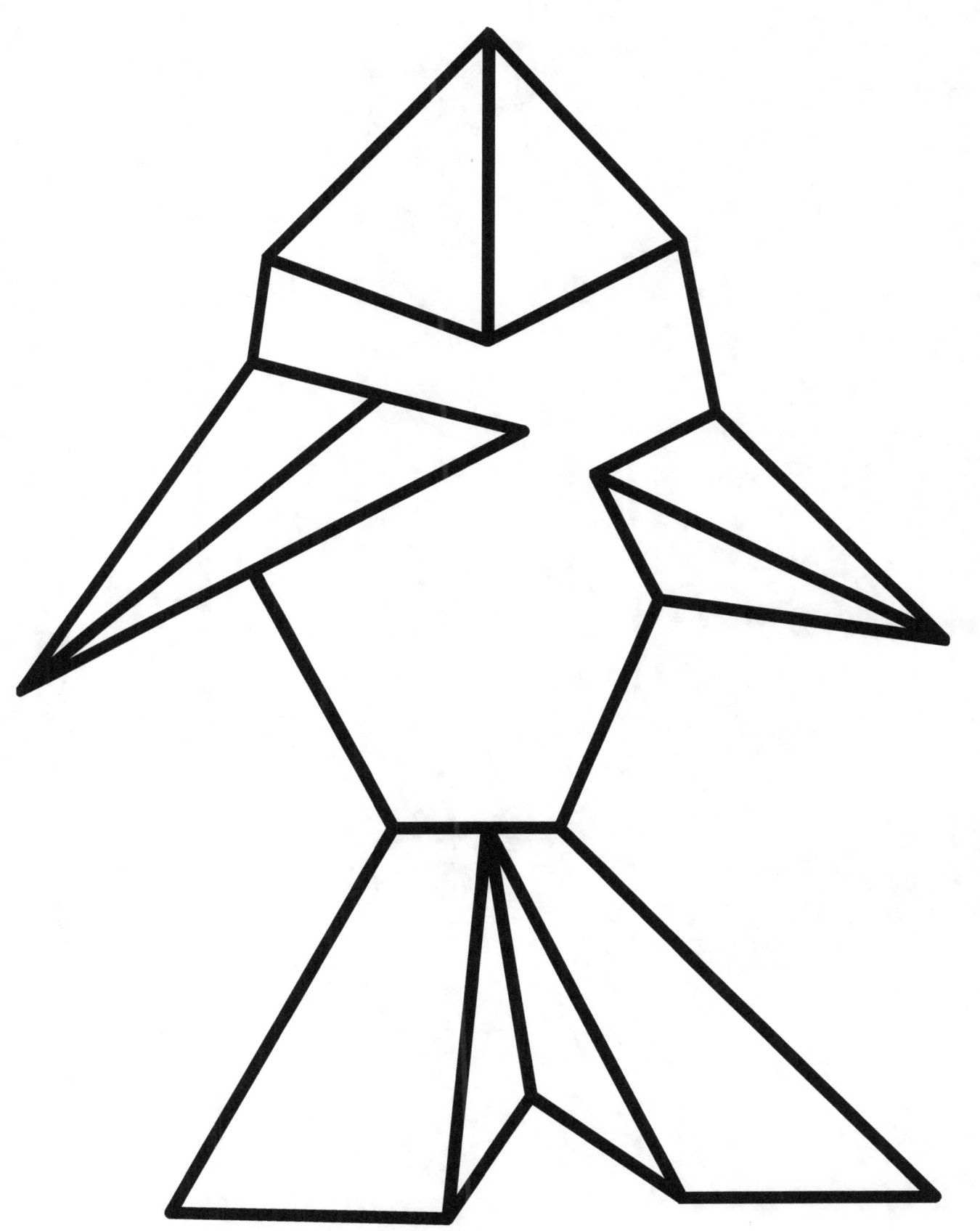

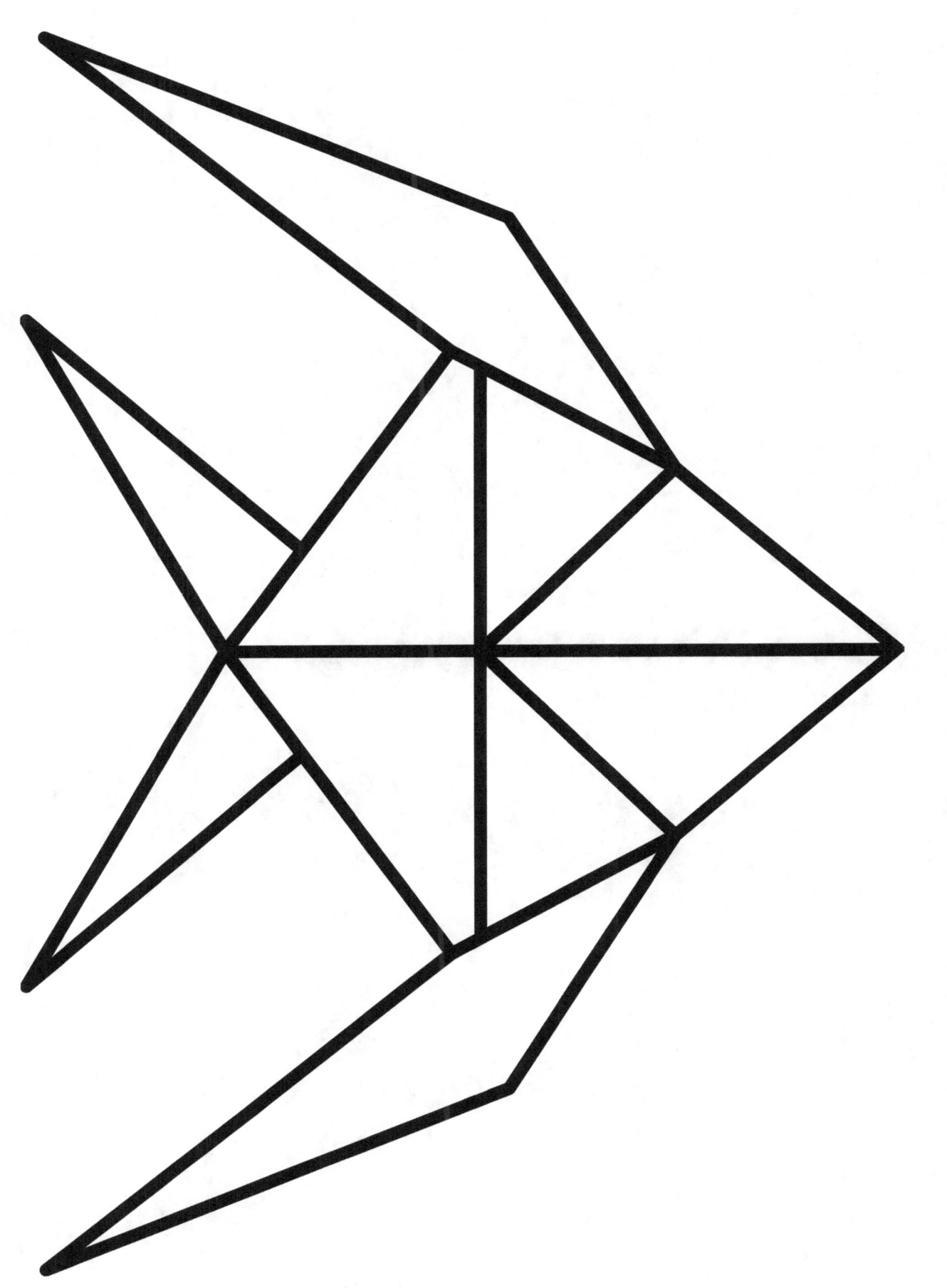

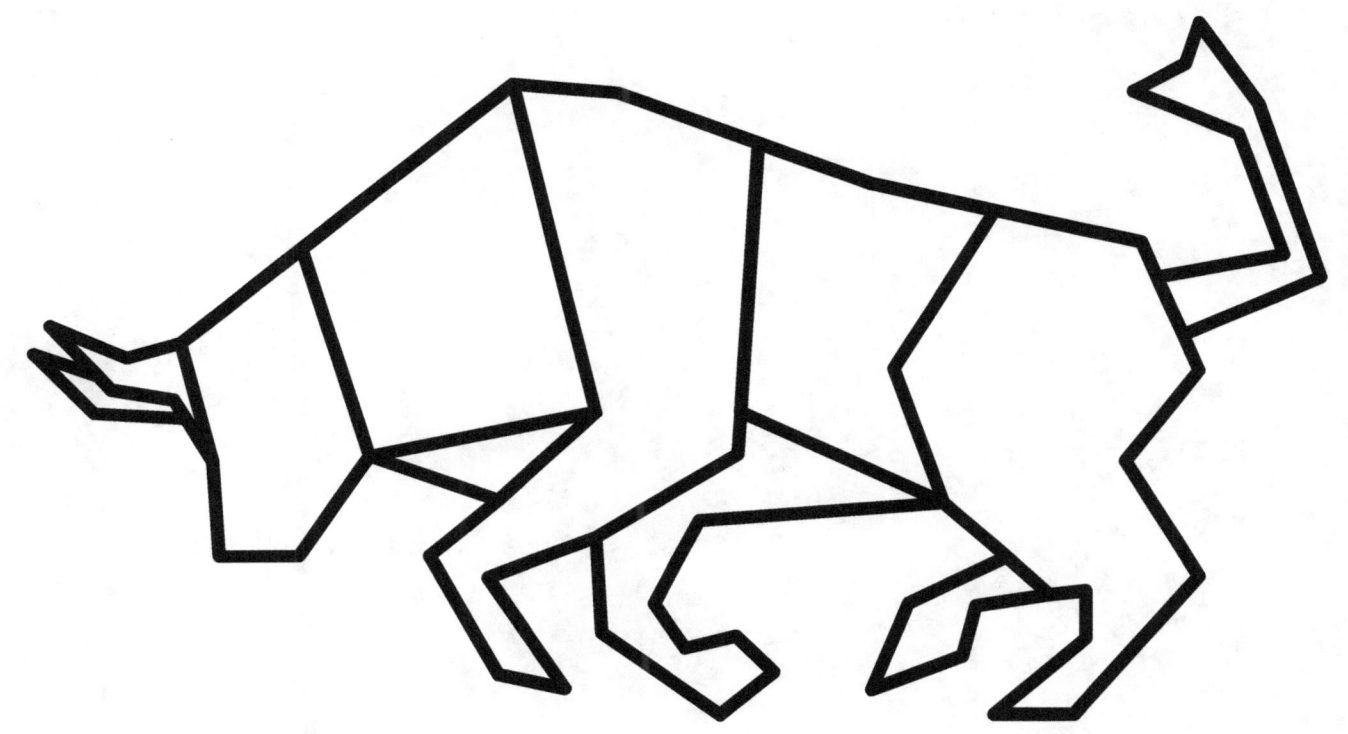

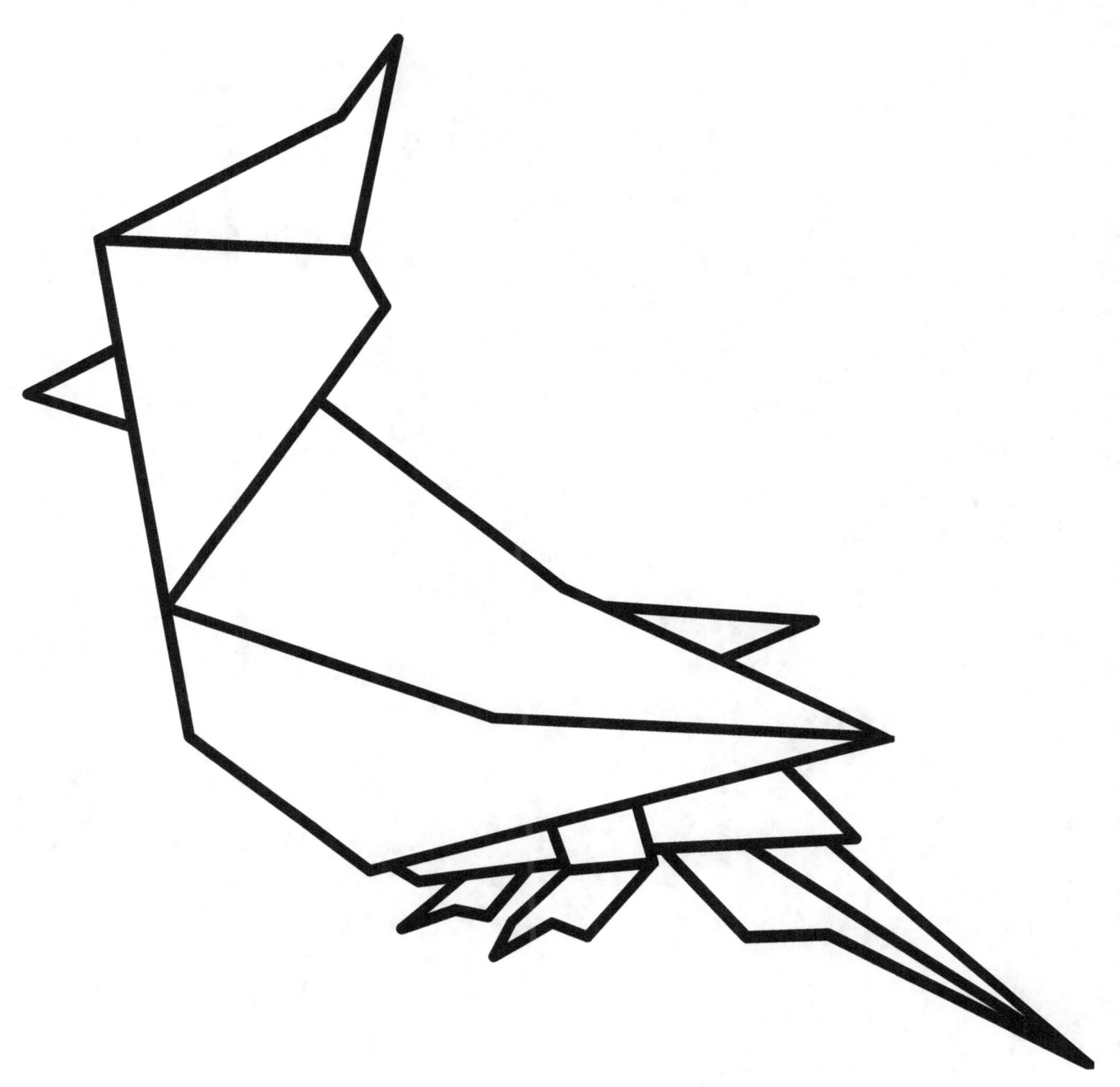

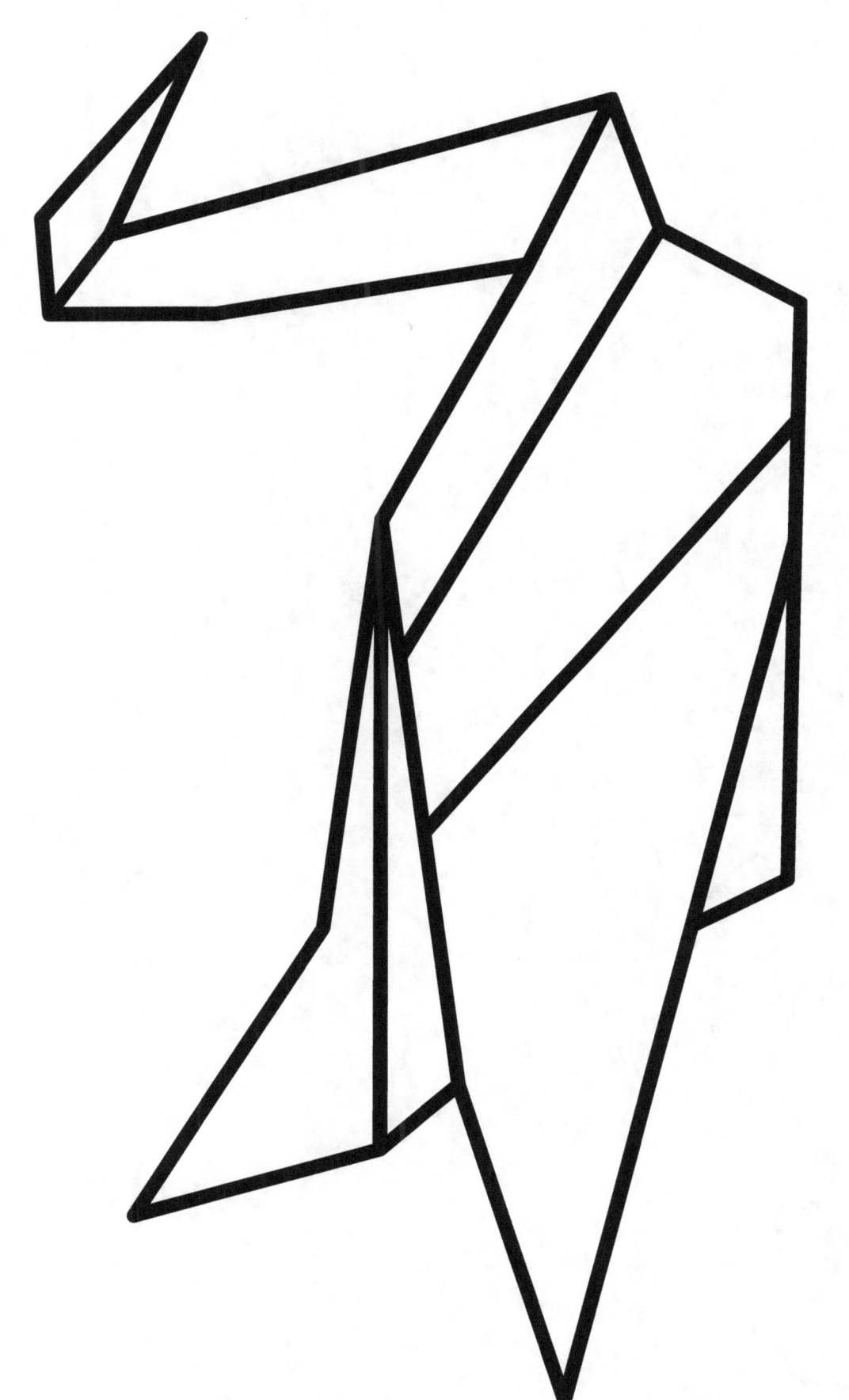

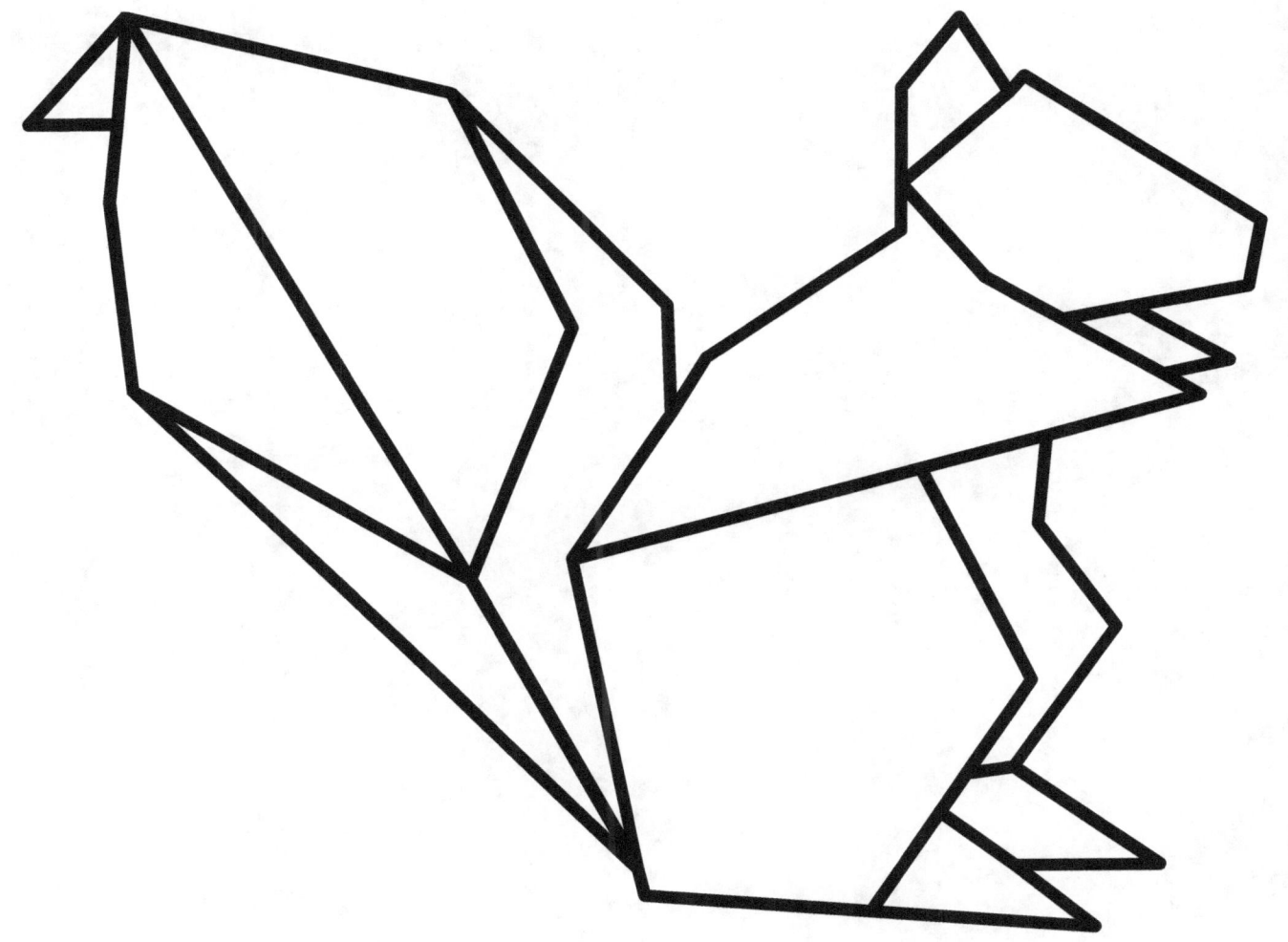

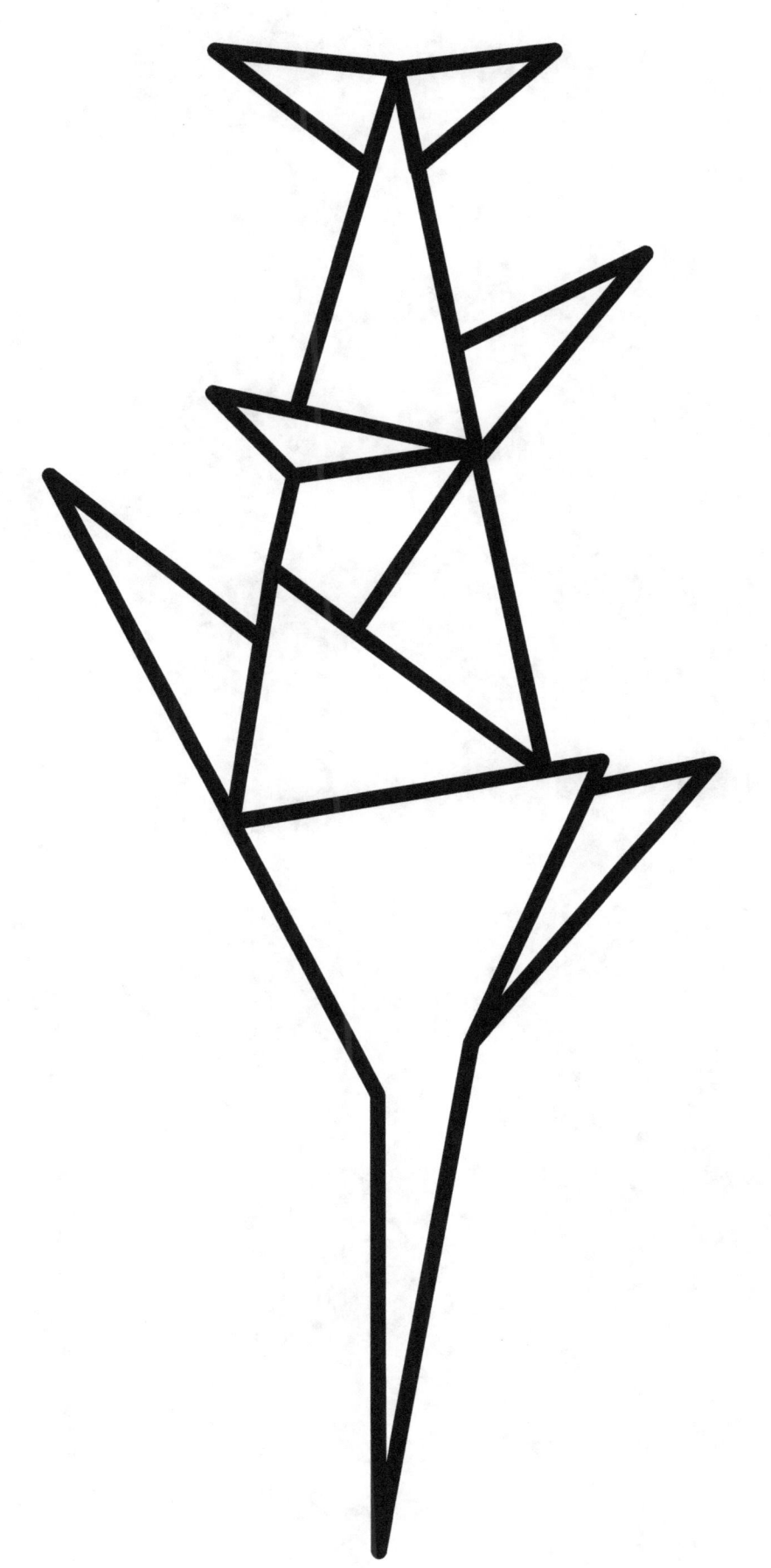

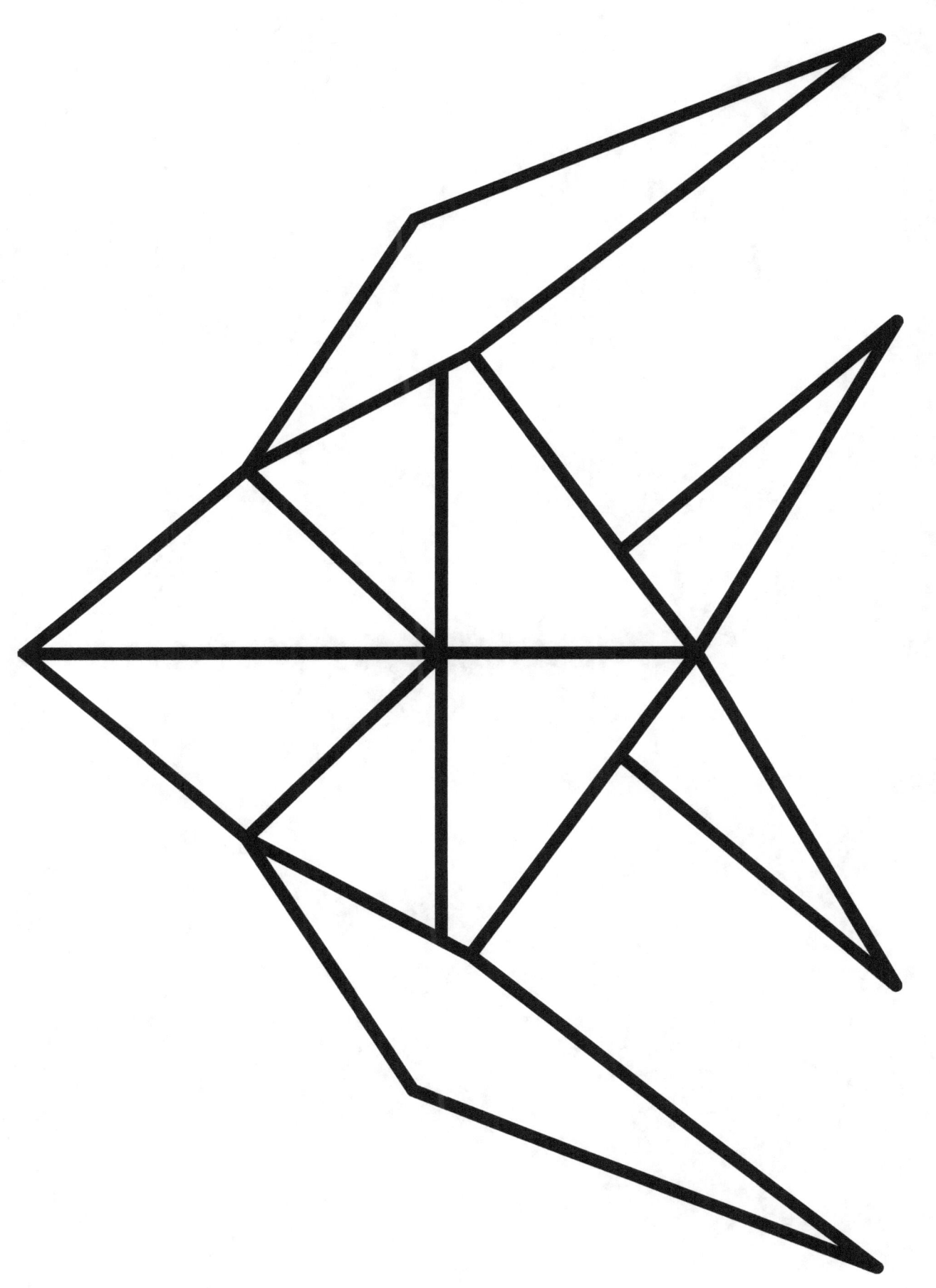

THE END!

That's the end of this fun book. But check out our other coloring books for even more fun!

Other coloring books:
Christmas Cat Coloring Book for Adults
50 Horses to Paint
Fun & Easy Animal Anatomy Coloring Book
The Christmas Dog Coloring Book
50+ Easy Flowers Coloring Book for Seniors

Happiness is the art of relaxation

Maxwell Maltz

www.ingramcontent.com/pod-product-compliance
Lightning Source LLC
Chambersburg PA
CBHW080621220526
45466CB00010B/3413